Dismantling the Twin Towers of Race and Racism:

A Vision of America's Way Forward

by the Rev. Alfred M. Walker, I

Searchlight Press
Dallas, Texas

Dismantling the Twin Towers
of Race and Racism:

A Vision of America's Way Forward

by the Rev. Alfred M. Walker, I

ISBN: 978-1-936497-12-6

No part of this publication may be reproduced, stored in a retrieval system, or transmitted by any means, except as permitted under Sections 107 or 108 of the 1976 United States Copyright Act without prior written permission of the publisher.

Scripture taken from the
KJV - Authorized Version (KJV) - 1769 Blayney Edition of the 1611 King James Version of the English Bible

RSV - The Holy Bible, Revised Standard Version 1952 (RSV), the authorized revision of the American Standard Version of 1901, Copyright © 1946, 1952, 1973 by the Division of Christian Education of the National Council of Churches of Christ in the United States of America.

Searchlight Press
Who are you looking for?
Publishers of thoughtful Christian books since 1994.
5634 Ledgestone Drive
Dallas, TX 75214-2026
888.896.6081
info@Searchlight-Press.com
www.Searchlight-Press.com

Manufactured in the United States of America

Table of Contents

Dedication	4
Acknowledgments	5
Foreword: Dr. Philip Dunston, Jr.	7
Introduction: Alfred M. Walker, I	9
Chapter 1 – The Guilty Stain	11
Chapter 2 – The Route to Redemption	25
Chapter 3 - Where is the God of Justice?	41
Chapter 4 - The Journey of Wise Men & Women	53
Chapter 5 - Spiritual Ears For Social Change	75
Chapter 6 - Spiritual Tongues for Social Change	91
Chapter 7 - Pharaoh Meets Great Jehovah – I	103
Chapter 8 - Pharaoh Meets Great Jehovah – II	115
Chapter 9 - Pharaoh Meets Great Jehovah – III	131
Chapter 10 - God's Choice of Freedom for Oppressed People	145
Next Steps: A Proactive Stance	163
About the Author	167

Dedication

To my wife and life partner, Angela, whose love and inspiration continue to affirm our lives together, our potential for responding to the love and call of God, and the challenge of becoming our best selves.

To our children, Azaria and Al Mark, whose lives have greatly enriched ours and our home. They are truly blessings from God.

To my daughter Aisha, who has grown to become a beautiful young lady. I continually thank God for her spirit and persistence in achieving her goals.

And lastly, to my mother Pauline Walker, whose love and strength have nurtured me my entire life. For this I am eternally grateful.

To these and my entire extended family I dedicate this work.

A special dedication to the memory of my father, the late Deacon Alfred Walker, Sr., whose faith and wisdom are forever before me

Acknowledgments

I am forever grateful to the pastors who have influenced and helped me shape my life and ministry: the late Rev. Preston Randall; the Rev. Dr. Arthur Sims; the Rev. Andrew Johnson; the late Rev. Berry Williams; and the late Rev. Dr. Roswell Jackson.

I shall never forget the professors, too numerous to name, who have forever enlightened my heart and mind.

Thank you to Mrs. Judith Davidson for her labor in transcribing most of the material. Much thanks and appreciation to Dr. Roland J. Hill for editing this work. His listening ear and encouraging word were invaluable. And to Dr. John Cunyus for his dedication in publishing this book, I am grateful

Also I am eternally indebted to the members of Liberty Baptist Church in Augusta, Georgia and New Hope Baptist Church in Dallas, Texas, for the privilege to the Preach the Gospel from those great pulpits.

Lastly, I am very grateful for the invaluable critique of the first two chapters (as research) of this work

Twin Towers, 6

provided by Dr. Cain Hope Felder of Howard University Divinity School

Foreword

Pastor Alfred M. Walker has addressed a critical area for the body of Christ as we embrace the 21st century. In his book, Dismantling The Twin Towers of Race and Racism, he has reawakened our awareness of this social construct and how it has impacted his life and the life of the church. His musings regarding his personal experiences with racism lend credibility to his passion and the need for the faith community to respond effectively to this stronghold that impacts the whole of human existence.

Pastor Walker is an insightful scholar and a powerful preacher of the gospel of Jesus Christ. His sermonic expressions regarding the life and times of Israel, Jesus the Christ and the Apostle Paul, not only highlight how they dealt with race and racism, but offer the church practical ways of exploring and teaching on this issue. Moreover, the body of Christ can extract useful tools on how we can speak truth to power and be healed from our wounds.

W.E.B. DuBois in his momentous work entitled, The Souls of Black Folk, (1903) stated that, "the problem of the twentieth century is the problem of the color line." Here we are, one hundred years later, and the same problem still exists. Alfred M. Walker has amply taken up this mantle and challenged the body of Christ to step up to the forefront and address the issue of race and racism in America. I highly recommend this book for pastors, teachers and all those who are called by God's name.

If we would humble ourselves, educate ourselves and address the wickedness of race and racism, I believe that God would heal our land. This book will rekindle the fire inside of you to take up the mantle and assist in the fight to eradicate injustice everywhere. If there was ever a time when the twin towers of race and racism needed to be dismantled, the time is now.

Dr. Philip Dunston Jr., Chair
Department of Religion and Philosophy
Clark Atlanta University

Introduction

> **"Race" not only identifies who one is and what one's heritage is, but invariably links one with his/her point of origin.**

It is my understanding that the term "race" refers to one's physical or physiological characteristics that distinguish one set of ethnic groups from another. It has to do with who one is based on one's ancestry. Hence, "race" is a social construct. It is therefore impossible to talk about race without talking about one's lineage. "Race" for persons within their own particular race, the term can carry a much more qualitative distinction. For persons outside a particular race, the term may serve only as a means of designating "others" whereas, those within a particular race see the term as a bond of identity and a connectedness to their community (who one really is).

This leads to my assertion that "race" not only identifies who one is and what one's heritage is, but invariably links one with his/her point of origin. It is for this reason that I choose to embrace Pan-Africanism. This school of thought according to Dr. N'Dugu Tofori Atta, retired professor of evangelism at the Interdenominational Theological Center in Atlanta, "is the coming to consciousness on the part of an individual concerning "who he/she is based in their ultimate truth of "whose one is."

Therefore my chief aim in writing <u>Dismantling The Twin Towers of Race and Racism</u> is twofold. First and foremost my attempt is to assist the Faith Community in discovering how to righteously address and respond to the issue of race and racism as a people of faith. We cannot afford to approach eradicating racism without the "Transforming Power" of the church. Secondly my hope is to reflect the loving justice of God as demonstrated in the life of Jesus the Christ and the Holy Scriptures by addressing these core issues facing America from a theological and moral perspective. It is my belief that there is a need to practically address and resolve the issue of racism.

Rev. Alfred M. Walker, I

The Guilty Stain

Twin Towers, 12

I was introduced, as little boy, to the twin towers of Race and Racism in the town of my boyhood, Augusta, Georgia. I remember an occasion when my mother took my brothers and me to the local swimming pool. The twin towers of race and racism cast a huge shadow in route to the pool that day as we watched two little black girls being taunted by a group of young white boys. The little girls cringed as the young white boys hurled racial slurs and ugly derogatory names against their tender innocent eardrums. My mother, a drum major for justice herself, bolted from the car and ran the boys off. Sadly, this was not an isolated incident, but a common experience I would come to face growing up as a Black youth during the 1950's and 1960's in Augusta, Georgia.

> **The little girls cringed as the young white boys hurled racial slurs and ugly derogatory names against their tender innocent eardrums.**

I was fortunate to have parents who instilled in my siblings and me pride for who we were and from whom we descended. But my parents were not alone in fortifying us with a good self-image for we were part of a civic and religious community that was intentional about fighting off the attacks of race and racism and interestingly enough it wasn't just from people of African decent. There were the White priests and nuns of the all Black Catholic School, Immaculate Conception Academy. Unlike other White Christians in our town who used their religion to fuel segregation, the White priests and nuns affirmed the "being" of our race. They were the leaven God used, at least for my part, to transcend the ugly realities of racism, which I would need as I entered junior high school.

In 1968, I was one of twelve Black students to integrate Langford Junior High, a school with an enrollment that exceeded 900. Racism became a reality to me then as I marched every day into a socially charged and hostile environment. Many White students resisted the idea of Blacks attending their school and openly and defiantly hurled racial slurs and played cruel mental games, which almost weekly resulted in some type of altercation or confrontation. We Black students were aware of Martin King's ethic of non-violence, but our frayed and youthful mental state couldn't and didn't embrace non-violence. We fought back!

The fight for social equality and against racial injustice continued in my adult years first as I entered the U.S. Navy and then in my first pastorate,

> **We Black students were aware of Martin King's ethic of non-violence, but our frayed and youthful mental state couldn't and didn't embrace non-violence. We fought back!**

ironically, back in my hometown of Augusta. There I was elected president of the local National Associations for the Advancement of Colored People (NAACP). Shortly after taking office, a young black man, trying to elude arrest by two white local Sheriff's, was shot and killed. The Black community believed, since the young man was unarmed, the shooting to be racially motivated. The tension in the community rose to almost riot stage as an all White jury acquitted the two White Sheriffs of any wrongdoing. It was my responsibility as president of the NAACP to help the Black Community sort through this apparent senseless death. The NAACP held press conferences, co-sponsored town-hall meetings, engaged the services of the U.S. Justice Department in a review of the case, and sat with the victim's family and attorney while the District Attorney was reviewing the case.

This case gave me an insider's look into the deep-seated prejudice that pervades our country, the festering hatred white people have for we brothers and sisters of a darker color, and it gave me a passionate commitment for helping dismantle race and racism in this country. I also recognized during this case that all Whites don't feel or act the same way. Like my teachers at Immaculate Conception Academy, there were those Whites who affirmed our "being" as people of African descent and furiously fought to dismantle the terrorist attacks of Jim Crow.

My involvement with the NAACP became my epiphany to the part the White Christian church played in perpetuating racist practices, and also the crucial role the Christian church as a whole must play in dismantling the twin towers of race and racism. There is heavy onus that the White Christian church in America carries in erecting and protecting racial injustice in this country. I agree with Dr. Mack King Carter when he states that many White Christians in this country "Americanized" the Christ of Nazareth. They have emasculated the liberator and made Christ into a patriotic Klansman.

In his book, <u>The Quest for Freedom: An African-American Odyssey</u>, Dr. Carter states that this "Americanized" Christ has resulted in "the abandonment of the tenets of the teachings of the biblical Christ and has made the White church more hypocritically patriotic than Christian".[1]

Carter's positing unearths the greatest threat to the Church; when Christians confuse culture with Christianity and are unenlightened to the truth, relevance, and liberating power of the Gospel of Jesus the Christ she becomes partakers of that culture's sins, and for American culture it would be the sins of race and racism.

American culture need not be racist. Dr. Gardner C. Taylor states, "the most precious words known to the human heart; liberty, justice, and freedom (are a part of our country's heritage)." [2]

These culture-shaping words, which were embraced by our founding fathers, should strike a deadly blow

> Like the former towers of the World Trade Center which stood to remind America of her international prowess, so does the protruding presence of race and racism continue to remind this country of her long history of oppression and hatred toward Native- Americans, African-Americans, and other people of color in this our land.

to the twin towers of race and racism. And yet, racism is still pervasive and widespread. Like the former towers of the World Trade Center which stood to remind America of her international prowess, so does the protruding presence of race and racism continue to remind this country of her long history of oppression and hatred toward Native- Americans, African-Americans, and other people of color in this our land. While we fight a war on terrorism abroad, which began shortly after the attack on New York's Twin Towers, we are haunted by the hypocritical past and presence of the vestiges of racial terrorism at home.

Though I love the United States of America and am proud to be one her citizens, I cannot and will not be silent about the lack of commitment on the part of politicians and preachers to the work of dismantling racism in this country. Apathy in dealing with this corrosive social issue is shown in American domestic economic policies. How does a country, unable to appropriate funds to bolster its educational system, somehow find and allocate billions of dollars to fund what many now believe to be an "unjust war"(the Iraq War)? How does a country unwilling to alleviate poverty and homelessness within her borders continue to invest in the possibility of life beyond this galaxy?

> **History shows that race and racism are inextricably bound to the fabric of this nation.**

It appears that while America reaches out to solve the world's problems, she refuses to acknowledge the protruding presence of the ominous twin towers of race and racism shown in her racist domestic policies and practices. It is paradoxical that while the nation is in a race to conquer outer space, the race question is still left unanswered. Our founding fathers, while drafting a document that at its core should have halted the construction of the twin towers, by their actions sanctioned the continued growth of racism in this country.

America from its inception has shown duplicity. While the Constitution and the Declaration of Independence declared equal rights for all, people of African decent were viewed as property. Africans in America were relegated to the position of "less than human" and refused their portion of life, liberty, and the pursuit of happiness. Even throughout the periods that established the Emancipation Proclamation, the days of Jim Crow, and the Civil Rights Era, America has never owned up to her "unholy" holy beginnings.

History shows that race and racism are inextricably bound to the fabric of this nation. The greatness of any nation is bound up in how she deals with her domestic problems. America's greatest domestic problem is race and racism. To reach her fullest potential, America must first own her past and present history of racial injustice, secondly, she must see racism as a major stain on America's stately royal robe and see that it is a major hindrance to her progress as a nation. Finally, America must forge ahead with a viable plan to dismantle the twin towers.

Derrick Bell, in his book, <u>Faces at the Bottom of the Well</u>, asserts that "the fabric of American society is such that racism will remain a permanent stain on American culture unless both Blacks as a whole and concerned Whites recognize the deep and relentless impact of racism on our nation"[3].

Bell believes that the only way to engage this country in the work of dismantling the twin towers is for America to come to grips with her dark and tragic past. His hope is that a good dose of reality would spark action among Blacks and Whites. He decries the history of race and racism that has caused many African Americans to believe either that they are no longer forces to be reckoned with or they were not forces at all.

Bell's observation does highlight the need for a loud and resounding wake-up call. Too many of us, Blacks and Whites, have been lulled to sleep with the lullaby of integration and are asleep to the grave issue of race and racism in this country. We settle for wishful dreams of eliminating racism, not understanding that dismantling the twin towers requires commitment and action. It requires, as Derrick Bell suggests, finding salvation in the struggle itself for an anti-racist society.

This is the work of both Blacks and Whites, for racism just doesn't impact Blacks. C. Eric Lincoln in his book, <u>Race, Religion, and the Continuing American Dilemma</u>, states, "the same fetters that bind the captive bind the captor, and the American people are captives of their own myths, woven so cleverly and so imperceptibly into the fabric of our national experience."[4]

The myths are so real that we have lost our identity. We no longer know who we are. I believe that the identity crisis brought on by racism in this country is at the core of the problem.

Whenever we broach the subject of race, we are really speaking of one's natural identity or physical make-up. It has to do with who one is, based on one's ancestry. Dr. Tofori Atta's earlier definition of race then, broadens the discussion of race. It helps us to understand that until one fully comes to embrace his/her race, and is thereby linked to their point of origin (God), he/she is unable to and in all likelihood unwilling to participate in and promote the larger context of community.

That is why I believe knowing one's identity is critical to create a document of racial reconciliation. It has been my experience that people who are not one with themselves and their Creator are those who likely become proponents of racism. Our founding fathers and even present day leaders refuse to acknowledge the common element of human beings; all were created in the image of God, and all were given the life-force (God's breath of life).

> **Racism is the painfully obvious admission that all Americans are not considered human beings.**

Racism is the painfully obvious admission that all Americans are not considered human beings. Our nation has always subjugated one group of people for the purpose of gain and power. The myths that have been promoted and perpetuated, on the part of Whites in this country, that of European entitlement and prominence, the very myth that C. Erick Lincoln characterized as enslaving both the captive and the captor. The manacles that bind the oppressed also bind the oppressors.

Orlando Bagwell, in his preface to the documentary, "Africans in America: America's Journey through Slavery" states, "Legal enslavement lasted in this land until the passage of the Thirteenth Amendment in 1865. For almost one hundred years after the American Revolution, slavery and freedom stood side by side. How could a nation that believed in the right to 'life, liberty, and the pursuit of happiness' justify the un-free status of millions of people within its boundaries?" [5]

Bagwell's point cuts to the quick, America had so diluted herself to believe she could vacillate between the diametrically opposed positions of freedom and slavery. Her leaders had convinced themselves that they were right in seeing themselves as privileged and superior.

It was in fact this false sense of identity that served as the impetus for racial and sexual distinctions being tolerated as a part of the norm. Bagwell asserts, "somewhere in the past we learned to accept inequality in our society, we developed a tolerance for notions of superiority and inferiority, and we began to subscribe to the notions of racial distinctions. It was during this stage of our history that we began to lose sight of our common identity."[6]

Even Christianity was used to reshape the common identity. Religious Whites accepted a distorted view of God that allowed them to believe that their skin color alone ordained them to a superior status while relegating Blacks to an inferior status. This confused identity was accomplished under the banner, "a nation under God."

This ungodly concept that God made some superior while he made others inferior is indeed a stain on our nation. Understanding the background of the building of the twin towers of race and racism in America convinces me that the dismantling of the problem of race and racism in American will require both an honest look our history and rethinking of our theology. This major work of dismantling the problem of race and racism will require an epistemological approach and a hermeneutical approach. It will take social thinking and ecclesiastical involvement.

Notes:
1. Mack King Carter, <u>The Quest for Freedom: An African-American Odyssey</u>,

Twin Towers, 24

2. Gardener C. Taylor, (Speech during Black History Month, Atlanta, 1072)
3. Derrick Bell, Faces at the Bottom of the Well, New York, NY: Basic Books, 1992. p. 62
4. C. Eric Lincoln, Race, Religion, and The Continuing American Dilemma, New York, NY:Hill and Wang, 1984, p. 3
5. Orlando Bagwell, Africans In America: America's Journey Through Slavery, New York, NY: Harcourt, Brace and Company, 1998. p. X
6. Ibid

The Route to Redemption

> **The very soul of the nation hinges on this redemptive racial reconciliation and, this racial reconciliation is directly tied to America's willingness to acknowledge, utilize, and teach lessons learned from her past transgressions.**

In the preceding chapter, I simply stated the problem; America's refusal to acknowledge how deep and abiding race and racism is in this country. In fact, though the founding fathers drafted a constitution of equality, the United States of America was actually established on principles of inequity, deceit, and dehumanization. What is crucial now for our country is that we draw up and implement a lucid redemptive route to dismantling the twin towers of race and racism.

The very soul of the nation hinges on this redemptive racial reconciliation and, this racial reconciliation is directly tied to America's willingness to acknowledge, utilize, and teach lessons learned from her past transgressions. This is a major task for many White Americans, because it is difficult, to say the least, to confess to being racist or to confess any benefits derived from racism.

Whites don't necessarily associate racism with privilege, but Beverly Daniels Tatum brings clarity to Whites' challenge of owning racism by tweaking the definition of racism. She writes that, "a loose definition of racism, such as prejudice plus power has little or no personal relevance for Whites. However, by utilizing David Wellman's definition of racism: 'A system of advantage based on race,' most White people, if they are really being honest with themselves, can see that there are advantages to being White in the United States. Despite the current rhetoric about affirmative action and 'reverse racism' every indicator, from slavery to life expectancy, reveals the advantage of being White."[1]

Yet, most White people claim ignorance about this ugly stain on American society. Looking squarely at the problem, the denial of the pervasiveness of racism in this country's past and present can no longer be afforded or tolerated. Our great nation must be willing to change her position as it relates to race and begin to respect and honor the human worth and dignity of every person residing within her borders. Not facing and not fixing this racial reality comes with a considerable consequence – ultimate demise of the most powerful and influential nation in the world.

Dr. Martin L. King Jr., triumphed this conviction, "We are all caught in an inescapable network of mutuality, tied to a single garment of destiny, what effects one man directly effects all men, indirectly."[2]

The United States of America can no longer fool herself into believing that the growing disparity between classes and races, the "haves" and "have nots" is not real or legitimate. Reality reveals that privileged Whites in this country continue to prosper while the majority of Americans live in diminished capacities. This must change, if redemptive reconciliation is to take place. Substantive change begins when Whites own up to their privilege status that comes merely because of the color of their skin.

Racism shows itself also through sexism. Bell Hooks, in her book <u>Ain't I a Woman</u>, purports that the issues of Black women have been misunderstood, misinterpreted, and overlooked since the days of slavery. Hooks believes that women of color need to make larger writing contributions to the issues of sexism not only as means of dealing with women's issues, but as a way of confronting racism as well. Hooks recognizes that a major problem in dealing with racism in America is the tendency to see sexism and racism as separate issues. Her research verifies that sexism and racism are inextricably bound to each other.

Hooks strikes a blow to White feminists by declaring them part of the problem. She declares their research findings

> **Black women in this country from slavery until our present times have been relegated to the bottom of the social order.**

presents distorted views of Black womanhood. In her book, she refutes in a scholarly fashion those distorted views. She proves without a doubt, that Black women in this country from slavery until our present times have been relegated to the bottom of the social order. Hooks intention is to help America understand that the double-edged sword of racism and sexism has cut through the experience of Black women leaving them fighting among their ranks with Black men, as well as the larger society of White women and men.

For Hooks, how Black women are viewed is due largely in part to the promotion of conventional thinking through the continued investment on the part of Whites in a system that only serves Whites. She suggests that the academic system in America is a particular deterrent to the establishment of an anti-racist, anti-sexist society. Hook insists that those who benefit from the vestiges of racism and sexism manage to be more subtle and elusive of being portrayed as racist and sexist. She agrees with Derrick Bell that the history of racism and sexism in this country has caused many of its citizens to either believe that they were no longer forces to be reckoned with or they were not forces at all.

The route to dismantling the twin towers of race and racism in America for both Tatum and Hooks is difficult and almost impossible. Nonetheless, I believe that the redemptive route will begin when the proponents/beneficiaries of racism admit the advantages they have received solely because of their race. Harlon L. Dalton, in his essay "What White Folks Must Do," states, "It is imperative that White folks accept joint ownership of America's race problem. But they must first unlearn the many ways in which they commonly disown the race problem."[3]

Dalton further states that, "this position deprives Whites of the opportunity to be moral agents and to participate in the cleansing of this nations great stain."[4]

Dalton's assessment of the problem lines up with what I believe is the first step in drafting a redemptive route for dismantling the twin towers and that is own up to the problem. But moving beyond race and racism requires more. It requires an understanding that race and racism are interlinked with other social ills.

Therefore, a commitment to make changes politically, economically, socially, and personally will be required. It will require us to think differently about others and ourselves. It will require us to ask questions about the values and kinds of relationships that we will need in order to create a sustainable nation.

Forging this redemptive route to racial reconciliation will be fraught with trials, storms, and even casualties, but we must not let them deter us from the goal. We must turn trials into triumphs, storms into stepping stones, casualties into courage that increase our faith and hope in God and in our future together as a great nation under God. There is a song, sung in the African American church that expresses the above sentiments,

> Though the storms
> keep raging in my life
> and sometimes its hard
> to tell the night from day,
> still that hope lies within is reassured
> as I keep my eye upon that distant shore,
> I know He'll lead me safely

> **The route to racial reconciliation begins with the nation both rethinking its false identity and owning its past racist practices.**

to that blessed place He has prepared.
And if the winds keep on blowing in my life,
my soul has been anchored in the Lord!

The route to racial reconciliation begins with the nation both rethinking its false identity and owning its past racist practices, but I believe that this can only be accomplished as the Christian church in America moves to the forefront of the movement.

Dr. Benjamin E. Mays, who led a group representing Catholics, Jews, and Protestants in an historic meeting held in Chicago in 1963, stated, "We come this week to think together, to work together, to pray together, and to dedicate ourselves to the task of completing the job which Lincoln began 100 years ago. We recognize that that we have had 100 years to make religion real in human relations and that we may not have another 100 years on our theological commitment. We did not seek world leadership, but the Second World War thrust it upon the United States. But leadership requires more than industrial might and military might. It requires that we practice at home what we attempt to sell to the world. So we are here because our consciences will not let us rest in peace until we implement more fully in deed what we expound in words. As long as we say we believe in God, the brotherhood of man, and the Declaration of Independence, we have no choice but to strive with might and mind to close the gap between theory and practice. Until we do this, we play a hypocritical role and wear an uneasy conscience." [5]

These were appropriate words for a conference whose purpose was to address how racism could be eradicated in churches, synagogues, and in society at large. Dr. Mays was hopeful, but almost a half-century later we have yet to realize that possibility. It is incumbent on this generation to take on the mantle of responsibility for creating a society where every person is respected and given the opportunity to become their best.

We can no longer afford, in this great country of ours, the hypocrisy of saying one thing and doing another. Since we espouse the brotherhood and sisterhood of all humankind, then we must move with dispatch to draft and implement this document that will dismantle the twin towers of race and racism.

The 1963 ecumenical conference drafted this appeal to the nation in its closing session, "We call upon all American people to work, to pray and to act courageously in the cause of equality and human dignity while there is still time to eliminate racism permanently and decisively, to seize the historic opportunity the Lord has given us for healing an ancient rapture in the human family, to do this for the glory of God." [6]

This grand appeal certainly suggests the possibility of living in an anti-racist society, but I believe it also implies that holistic health and well-being are God's intention for all humankind. Therefore when we strive to achieve racial reconciliation, we in fact glorify God in the process. Drafting and implementing a redemptive racial route is in reality the work of the Christian church.

If this nation is to experience the healing brought about by the removal of the ominous twin towers of race and racism, it will be because God-fearing, conscientious citizens become active participants in the healing process.

Dr. Robert M. Franklin, in his book, <u>Another Day's Journey: Black Churches Confronting the American Crisis</u>, states, "My thesis is that the renewal of

American civil society depends on vigorous religious groups doing their part to heal, reconcile, nurture, guide, discipline, and inspire individuals to join in authentic community." [7]

Authentic communities can only be realized by those who believe in the power of reconciliation and healing, discipline and inspiration, and only people of Faith can lead a community to this type of authenticity. When the religious community takes its rightful leadership role in dismantling the twin towers of race and racism, our country will be a great nation. A nation that leads the world in truth, liberty, and justice. A nation that has accepted her ultimate challenge to be God's light to the world. A nation who sings with optimism,

There's a bright side, somewhere;
There's a bright side, somewhere.
Don't you stop until you find it;
There's a bright side, somewhere.

Notes:
1. Beverly Daniels Tatum, Defining Racism: Can We Talk?, New York, NY: Worth Publishers, 2001, p. 103.
2. Martin L. King, Jr., Sermon, *A Knock At Midnight*.
3. Harlon L. Dalton, What White Folks Must Do, New York, NY: Worth Publishers, 2001, p. 616.
4. Ibid. 262
5. Benjamin E. Mays, Born to Rebel, New York, NY: Charles Scribner's Sons, 1971, p. 262

Twin Towers, 36

6. Ibid. 262
7. Robert M. Franklin, <u>Another Day's Journey: Black Churches Confronting the American Crisis</u>, Minneapolis, MN: Fortress Press, 1997, p.124

Prophetic Messages to Prepare the Faith Community for its role in Dismantling the twin towers of Race and Racism

This grand appeal certainly suggests the possibility of living in an anti-racist society, but I believe it also implies that holistic health and well-being are God's intention for all humankind. Therefore when we strive to achieve racial reconciliation, we in fact glorify God in the process. Drafting and implementing a redemptive racial route is in reality the work of Christian church.

> **If this nation is to experience the healing brought about by the removal of the ominous twin towers of race and racism, it will be because God-fearing, conscientious citizens become active participants in the healing process.**

If this nation is to experience the healing brought about by the removal of the ominous twin towers of race and racism, it will be because God-fearing, conscientious citizens become active participants in the healing process. In the following chapters are ministerial musings that seek to give instruction and encouragement to the faith community about our role in the dismantling of the twin towers.

These chapters are designed to give a biblical

framework for the faith community's rationale for stepping to the plate of this major social concern. These messages were first presented at my church, New Hope Baptist Church, a church with a legacy of involvement in the civil rights movement and a church still located in the heart of the inner city.

Twin Towers, 40

Notes

Twin Towers, 41

Where is the God of Justice?

Twin Towers, 42

> **When tragedy strikes as it did September 11, 2001, in these United States of America, inevitably the question is raised: Where is God in all of this?**

Fire burns! Suffering hurts! Nevertheless, God is actively involved in the history of humankind, continually working all things together for good - even suffering - for those who love Him and are called according to His purpose. For the good of His people, God would come as a refiner's fire. The hurt and anguish resulting from September 11th's deplorable acts of violence will certainly reside with us for some time to come, but ultimately we as a church and nation will be better because of it.

When tragedy strikes as it did September 11, 2001, in these United States of America, inevitably the question is raised: Where is God in all of this? Catastrophe has a way of shaking us at the very core of our being. When thousands of lives are lost in one fell swoop, or when danger abides as an unwanted overnight guest, or when perpetrators of evil acts go unpunished, we question God's position in the matter. It was this same issue the prophet Malachi faced as he penned his poignant, prophetic words that we will consider in our text.

Malachi was called to prophesy during one of the most difficult periods of Israel's history. The time was one of deferred hopes and delayed promises. The prophets before Malachi had predicted the Lord would return in glory to His Temple. Haggai records these words in Verse 8 of Chapter 1: "Go up to the mountain, and bring wood, and build the house; and I will take pleasure in it, and I will be glorified, saith the Lord."

However, although the Temple had been rebuilt for more than half a century, no sign of the Lord's return had appeared. The prophets had also predicted that the Lord would bless the land with prosperity, but the people still found themselves the victims of abject and relentless poverty. There was such desperation that some of them were forced to sell their children into slavery. Unemployment was widespread throughout the land, for "there was no wage for man or any wage for beast," according to Zechariah 8:10.

Malachi's age was one of religious skepticism and indifference. A half-century of poverty and oppression had produced a dangerous reaction on the part of the Jews. The Jews' faith of former days had given way to doubts concerning God's goodness and justice. A new temper controlled the Jewish mind, and many persons had begun to sit "in the seat of the scornful." The land was ripe for judgment.

Leading up to the fateful and fatal September 11, 2001, it appears that America was ripe for judgment just like the people of God in Malachi's day. We witnessed in the decade prior to 9/11 the ugly and unrighteous purposes of a few misguided persons and how they produced disaster and mayhem. From the 1993 bombing of the same World Trade Center to the Oklahoma City bombing in 2000, we witnessed the devastation visited upon innocent victims and their families.

One need not even mention the unbelievable course of events involving our youth in awkward and pessimistic attempts to respond to their emotional life crises. From March 24, 1998, in Jonesboro, Arkansas, to September 15, 1999, in Fort Worth, Texas, we saw and heard of random acts of violence perpetrated by youthful offenders. All of this in my humble opinion suggests that this land was indeed ripe for judgment!

Yes, "Where is the God of justice?"

When Malachi stood up to announce the imminent arrival of the Day of Judgment, he began by accusing the people of having wearied the Lord with their words. The prophet shared the Old Testament view of the power and importance of speech. Speech has always been a reliable gauge of a person's character and personality. In a profound sense, we are what our speech reveals us to be.

> **How does a "Nation Under God" come from such a wretched past?**

The character of this country has been judged by the words contained in those documents that were used as the building blocks of this nation. The Constitution and the Declaration of Independence have allowed this country from its inception to say one thing and do another. Africans in America, relegated to "less than human" positions, built this country while never realizing their portion of life, liberty, and the pursuit of happiness. And even throughout the periods following the Emancipation Proclamation, the days of Jim Crow, and the Civil Rights Era, America has never owned up to her "unholy" holy beginnings.

How does a "Nation Under God" come from such a wretched past? How does a country unable to appropriate funds to bolster its educational system somehow find billions of dollars to fund a "war" of nonsense in order to eradicate one dark-skinned man? How can a country unwilling to alleviate poverty and homelessness within her own ranks be so willing to invest in the possibility of life beyond this galaxy? She does it by justifying the inconsistencies between her character and her speech.

How offensive we can be at times, even with our words concerning God. In one of his speeches, President Bush stated that our nation was now at war with the terrorists and terrorist sympathizers of the world. As if waging war of that scope and magnitude wasn't enough, he officially named the military effort "Operation Infinite Justice." How could the President and the military of a "Nation Under God" ever refer to any human endeavor as being infinite? To brandish that word "infinite" is tantamount to dethroning God Almighty. Could this be what we were witnessing in this country?

Rather than taking the time to become more vigilant and wise, many in this nation were screaming for retaliation and vengeance, forgetting that vengeance belongs to God. We need to be a nation that shores up and rebuilds her damaged institutions; guards her borders; tightens her internal security; and locks arms with other nations who seek freedom and justice. We need to be careful not to flex our "militaristic muscle." That offends God.

The offending words against God by the Jews were spoken in the form of a question. They asked, "Where is the God of Justice?"

The question was not designed to obtain information about God's whereabouts, but to launch a complaint against Him. At the heart of the complaint was a denial that God was involved actively in the affairs of history. But nothing could be further from the truth. In the Old and New Testament, God is pictured as working at the center of history and guiding it toward its ultimate goal. Throughout Scripture, God continually refuses to leave His ultimate outcome in the hands of evil people. Therefore, to deny His active involvement in history is to deny His existence. And so for those who question the existence of and ability of God by asking, "Where is the God of Justice?" Malachi warned that they would soon discover God's weighty answer to a defiant question.

Notice first that God would come as a refiner's fire to burn away all of Israel's dross. Malachi 3:2-3. The refiner's fire suggests refining and purifying. Silver and gold are of little value unless they have passed through the refiner's fire. As silver and gold passes

> **The Bible teaches that God sometimes allows suffering and trials to overwhelm us in order that we may be purified and prepared for more effective service.**

through the refiner's furnace, the fire burns away the impurities, but leaves the precious metals. That which is true of metal holds true for individuals and nations. We cannot render acceptable service to God if our lives have not been refined and purified. Isaiah warned that the Lord rejected Jerusalem because her silver had become dross and her wine had been diluted with water.

The question that our text evokes then is, "But what about the fiery trials that come our way?"

The Bible teaches that God sometimes allows suffering and trials to overwhelm us in order that we may be purified and prepared for more effective service. Paul's "thorn in the flesh" is a good example of this kind of suffering. It was his "thorn in the flesh" that taught him to rely more on God and less on himself. Paul reflected on this lesson in his letter to the church at Philippi. He declared that God used the trials he endured while in Rome for the advancement of the gospel.

The trials that God allows His children to endure must never be interpreted as a denial of His love for us. In some circumstances, the trials may be seen on the contrary as proof of His love. James wrote to Christians who faced heavy trials: "Count it all joy, my brethren, when you meet various trials, for you know that the testing of your faith produces steadfastness. And let steadfastness have it full effect, that you may be perfect and complete, lacking in nothing." James 1:2-4.

The author of the book of Hebrews went a step further when he affirmed that suffering as a form of discipline gives proof that God loves us and accepts us as His children. In the twelfth chapter of Hebrews he wrote, "But God disciplines us for our good, that we may share his holiness. For the moment all discipline seems painful rather than pleasant; later it yields the peaceful fruit of righteousness to those who have been trained by it." Hebrews 12:10-11.

Fire burns! Suffering hurts! Nevertheless, God is actively involved in the history of humankind, continually working all things together for good – even suffering – for those who love Him and are called according to His purpose. For the good of His people, God would come as a refiner's fire. The hurt and anguish resulting from deplorable acts of violence on September 11 will certainly reside with us for some time to come, but ultimately, we as a church and nation will be better because of it.

Lastly, the text says He would come as "fuller's soap." Malachi 3:2. "Fuller" is an ancient term that was used to describe someone who laundered clothes by hand. The soap the fullers used in biblical times was prepared with lye obtained from the ashes of certain plants that grew along the shores of the Dead Sea. Even in our own history, we can recall grandmother and great-grandmother making lye soap from the potash that had been leached out of the ashes of certain types of woods.

Lye soap was tough on the hands, but it was very effective in removing dirt and stains from clothing. God's purpose in judgment was not only to burn away the dross of sin but to wash away its filthy stain. The people needed to have their sins removed so that they could offer acceptable sacrifices to the Lord, offerings that conformed to God's standards. I hear the elders singing,

> *There is a fountain filled with blood,*

*drawn from Emmanuel's veins,
and sinners plunged beneath that flood,
lose all their guilty stains.*

In every age, God's goal for His servants is that they should offer acceptable worship and service to Him. How this becomes a reality is recorded in Romans 12:1-2. Paul says, "I appeal to you therefore, brethren, by the mercies of God, to present your bodies as a living sacrifice, holy and acceptable to God, which is your reasonable service. Do not be conformed to this world, but be ye transformed by the renewing of your mind, that you may prove what is the will of God, what is good and acceptable and perfect."

> **Where is the God of justice? God is in the world working things out through humanity, so as to bring about His chief concern and ultimate will for our lives and the redemption of souls.**

No acceptable worship and/or service is possible apart from a full commitment to Him who is the object of our worship and service. Anything else is a sham and a pretense.

Twin Towers, 52

Where is the God of justice? God is in the world working things out through humanity, so as to bring about His chief concern and ultimate will for our lives and the redemption of souls. I hear the elders singing again,

I serve a risen Savior,
He's in the world today;
I know that He is living,
whatever others say;
I see His hand of mercy,
I hear His voice of cheer,
and every time I need Him,
He's always near.
He lives! He lives! He lives!

Amen!

The Journey
of Wise Men & Women

> **Life is a journey, some call it a journey from the cradle to the grave; nonetheless, it is a journey.**

"After Jesus was born in Bethlehem in Judea, during the time of King Herod, wise men from the east came to Jerusalem and asked, 'Where is the one who has been born king of the Jews? We saw his star in the east and have come to worship him.'" Matthew 2:1,2.

I believe the wise men in this text, while primarily meaning those ancient seekers of the Messiah, represent all true seekers of truth and justice. These ancient magi represent today's wise men and wise women who include children as well.

Life is a journey, some call it a journey from the cradle to the grave; nonetheless, it is a journey. The wise men from the east symbolize to us the journey of life. This real life pilgrimage is different from day to day. We might believe that life's journey will always run over roads that are smooth and paved. But reality brings us into check as we pass over many roads with potholes, twists, and turns. Life is a difficult journey but can be at its best when made by wise men and women.

These men from the east represented in the text were probably from Persia. They were multi-talented and multi-faceted which accounted for their wisdom. We don't know whether they were scientists and/or astrologers, but what we do know is that they were seekers of truth. They knew that truth and the essence of life resided beyond themselves; therefore, they left their home country in the east and journeyed west all the way to Jerusalem, then to Bethlehem, in search of truth.

The journey of wise men and women today is a journey that moves beyond the right now, it moves beyond who we are, it moves beyond the essence of personal limited understanding. The journey of life can never be calculated and/or restricted within the confines of what one is able to fathom. The confounding truth is that the journey of life is beyond the scope of all human reasoning.

The journey of wise men and women of African descent can be anchored in the journey of the wise men of the east. They were in search of wisdom. At the window of the nativity scene, we peer in and discover, as depicted by the wise men, an understanding of wisdom.

Wisdom cannot be gained from books. Wisdom cannot be gained by long times of study and/or reading. Wisdom according to James is a gift from God. "If any of you lack wisdom, let him ask of God, that giveth to all men liberally, and upbraideth not; and it shall be given him." James 1:5.

In today's plain English, James is saying, "if there is anyone who wants wisdom and seeks wisdom, he must turn to God, the only true source of wisdom." In my childhood, I heard the elders speak of wisdom in these terms, "motherwit," or just plain "commonsense."

What the wise men of the east reveal is that wisdom will take you a long way. Solomon's prayer becomes a prerequisite for men and women who seek wisdom. "Give therefore thy servant an understanding heart to judge thy people, that I may discern between good and bad: for who is able to judge this thy so great a people? 1 Kings 3:9.

His request pleased God resulting in wisdom and wealth for his life's journey. Wise men and women understand that wisdom will help you make the journey.

As we continue peering through the window of the nativity scene, the magi from the east teach us that God initiates the journey of wise men and women. The journey begins with God. The wise men didn't strike out on the journey on a hunch or a rumor but the scripture says they saw a star. The star became their guidance system to find the Messiah. Some say the star was an astrological sign; I contend it was a light from heaven. It was a beacon that led them from their homeland to the place of the birth of Christ. God used the star to begin their journey. He may not use a star to begin our journey but you can rest assured the God initiates the journey of wise men and women.

> **Understand that the beginning of man's journey began in Eden but was initiated by God who thought enough of us to create us in his image.**

Wise men and women know that people of all racial backgrounds began their journey thousands of years ago in the Garden of Eden, which has been identified in East Africa. Anthropologists and archeologists believe that humankind migrated from East Africa southward along the Nile into the area known today as Mesopotamia; then further north, east and west.

Understand that the beginning of man's journey began in Eden but was initiated by God who thought enough of us to create us in his image. The findings of Sir Henry Rawlinson, a noted Assyriologist, concludes that the Sumerian culture, the earliest culture to exist in Mesopotamia, was brought there by people from Africa. This conclusion confirms the biblical indication that Cush, whose name means "black," was the father of Nimrod the builder of Asshur, which is known today as Mesopotamia. Many scholars conclude that the journey of all people begins with people of color. To be clear on this historical journey, follow me through these facts.

The lineage of humankind began with God's miraculous creation of Adam. Apostle Paul elucidating this homogenous journey wrote, "And hath made of one blood all nations of men for to dwell on all the face of the earth." Acts 17:26.

The linkage of the races is seen again as one family survives the flood and humankind begins anew through the sons of Noah. From the lineage of these sons, particularly Ham, we see the development of great cities. Read Genesis 10:6-14, recorded are these facts about Cush and Nimrod. These brothers, men of color, built not jut Asshur, but the scripture documents Nimrod as the architect and builder of Nineveh.

From Noah's son Shem came Abraham the great patriarch that answered the call of God and migrated from the Chaldeans in Mesopotamia to the land of Canaan (Palestine) around 2000 B.C. When Abraham arrived in Palestine it's not surprising that he discovered that there were brothers and sisters of a darker hue already in the land. Yes, when Abraham reached the promise land, there were the Hivites, the Arkites, the Sidonians, the Hethites, the Jebusites, the Amorites, the Girgashites, the Hivites, the Arkites, the Sinites, and the Arvadites, all descends of Noah through his son Ham. The name Ham means "black" which permits us to conclude that the Canaanites, Ham's children were people of color.

From Canaan, Abraham's family migrated to Egypt. The story goes like this: Abraham fathered Isaac; Isaac fathered Jacob; Jacob fathered twelve sons who around 1800 B.C. migrated to Egypt to flee a famine in their country. When Jacob and his twelve sons and their family arrived in Egypt, can you guess what race of people greeted them? You are right. Once again it was people of color. Prior to the arrival of the Greeks in and around the fourth century B.C. there were

> He discovered men and women of color who had advanced knowledge in astrology, math, and architecture.

already people called Kenites inhabiting the land. They too were people of color.

Understand this that the Kenites were not unlearned cavemen, but highly intelligent people who educated the migrating family of God. Note that the presence of Europeans in Egypt and Palestine did not occur until Alexander the Great conquered or invaded Egypt in the 4th Century B.C. What Alexander the Great discovered was not unclothed and uncivilized natives, but a race of highly developed people. He discovered men and women of color who had advanced knowledge in astrology, math, and architecture. These were the people who had already built the pyramids, conquered many of the world's great mysteries, and protected and disseminated their findings and knowledge in the world's greatest library located in Alexandria.

For four hundred years the Israelites absorbed the learning of Egypt, from the Egyptian customs and culture to artisans skills, and the deep sciences from the first known universities. But it was not just learning that took place, Bishop Alfred Dunston in his book, <u>Black Men in the Old Testament and Its World</u>, writes that the Israelites that left Egypt during the great exodus were a mixed multitude.

Do the math. You read in Genesis that 70 Israelites went into Egypt at the time of the famine, four hundred years later over one million strong, not including women and children march out of Egypt. Seventy went in and four hundred years later one million came out. That tells me that not only did a group of Egyptians follow them out of Egypt but Israel came out with some Egyptian blood in them. God initiated the journey of Israel into Egypt to prove again that He is the God of all creation and that in God all men are brothers.

When Rome conquered the world around the 1st Century, it appeared that God was not a part of the journey. But God's guiding star caught the attention of wise men from the east, men of color, who came to welcome the birth of the Christ Child who became the beginning of a new journey in Christ, proving once again that the journey of wise men and women begins with God.

God is the beginning of all life: both earthly and eternal. God is the progenitor of all of life and if we are to understand the journey of wise men and women, we must begin with God. We African Americans, though displaced by the horrible Atlantic slave trade, must never forget that whatever we do, wherever we go, and whatever we achieve we do it because God initiated our journey. The old timers use to sing this song, "it's another day's journey and I'm glad about it."

We ought to be glad about our day's journey, our month's journey, and our years long journeying because they are microcosms of the real journey. And the real journey is the journey begun by God that leads to Christ.

Notice that the wise men of the east went in search of Christ, that tells me something. The journey of wise men and women will always lead to Christ. What good is it to be great? What good is it to ascribe to the best in life, whether food, entertainment and/or enjoyment? What good is it to visit the hallowed halls of sacred institutions of higher learning? What good is it to matriculate in the best Ivy League schools, if you don't seek Christ? What good is it if you speak with the tongues of angels and yet don't seek Christ? What good is it to vacation on the Riviera if you haven't sought Jesus? What good is it to know the taste of Boluga Caviar or the best pig's feet you've ever known (hopefully you can still remember the taste the pig feet) without the God who begins our journey?

Understand, wise men and women know without Christ we can do nothing. Without Christ we are empty vessels, sounding brass, void of real life. Therefore, we like the wise men of the east must be able to raise the question, where is He? We've seen the star. We've come to worship Him. Where is he? That's the question of wise men and women, where is Christ?

Every person needs to ask where is He, for He has already come and many of us are unaware of it. It is evident in the social milieu of our times. We have become preoccupied with self, worldly affairs, what's happening on Pennsylvania Avenue, and what's going on every where else, while forgetting about the one who began our journey. I am by no means saying that we should relinquish our concern about social, cultural, and political issues, but what I am suggesting is that wise men and women understand that these issues will only be resolved as we seek the Christ.

Raising the question of where is He, cuts to the very foundation of social ills. So wise men and women should raise this Christological question at unexpected times. In our behavior we ought to exude, where is he? Where is he who is born king of the Jews? In executive boardrooms full of corporate leaders the non-verbal question should be raised, where is He? In our courtrooms where the question of justice and inequality for all people is being debated, where is He must be felt.

But we as a nation and we as people of African decent have, by enlarge, ceased raising the question. The question has been muted by our social, economic, and political progress. Affluence has moved us away from God and sealed our lips. We don't seek the God who has brought us from a mighty long way. How sad, for we African American have been a resilient people. Our history records that no one has been able to conquer us; no one has been able to snuff us out. Talk about the holocaust, our forefathers experienced a holocaust unlike any race of people in human history, some estimate that more than 100 million African slaves died in the middle passage.

But we have allowed integration and prosperity to take our eyes off the God who began our journey. Wise men and women every now and then need to remember that God initiated our journey with the purpose of directing us to truth. We need to seek Christ. We ought to periodically move beyond ourselves. We ought to be willing to give of ourselves in selfless living. The baby that attracted wise men from the east, modeled the life we are to live. "God so loved the world that He gave His only begotten son."

God gave his son. The son gave his life.

We must move beyond ourselves in order to make changes in our world. We must be willing to deny ourselves, understanding that denial only comes by seeking Christ.

The wise men from the east discovered that seeking God caused a disturbance. John records the reaction of the world to the birth of Christ,
> *He was in the world, and the world was made by him, and the world knew him not. He came unto his own, and his own received him not.* John1:10,11.

Wise men and women ought to realize that seeking after Christ will disturb that which is normative. Be it known that those who seek Christ disturb the world. In Matthew's record of the birth of Christ, he paints with quick strokes how many people were disturbed

> **Know that your seeking the truth will disturb others**

because the wise men asked the question, where is he.

The Jews had expected a king not a humble child born in a stable. They expected a king not a Savior who identified with the least of these, the marginalized, and those who sit on the periphery always looking in. They expected a king not a Savior born into the world. They had no concept of God being born and coming down through forty and two generations. They expected a king but they certainly didn't expect a king of humility.

The wise men's question, where is he?, sent a ripple throughout Palestine. The government was disturbed, Herod was disturbed, the religionists were disturbed, the Sanhedrin was disturbed, the Pharisees and Sadducees were disturbed, because the magi raised the question that pointed to the birth of the King of Kings.

Know that your seeking the truth will disturb others. Herod's fears were unfounded. He would have long been dead by the time the baby born in Bethlehem could have reigned as king of the Jews. But nonetheless this grown man, this tyrant who history records as having murdered his own family, his brothers, his wives, was so disturbed he attempted to murder the messiah. When you seek the truth, you will disturb.

Wise men and women know that God initiates their journey. We know that our journey is about seeking truth. We understand that we must seek truth no matter what we hear, no matter how popularized or glamorized life and/or work around us may appear. We must never deviate from truth. My admonition is simple, never let anyone sway you from truth. Always seek truth. Be clear in your agenda that wise men and women' s journey is initiated by God, this journey seeks after Christ with the purpose of finding truth.

Finally, wise men and women see their journey centered around worship. Note I did not say the journey is consumed by worship, but centers around worship. What this means is that the beginning and end of our week is anchored in worship. We start the week and end the week in worship. The lives of those who are wise know that worship is integral to life.

Wisdom can never be attained without worshiping the one who gives wisdom. That's why the lives of the truly wise men and women are centered around worship. Matthew records that when the wise men found the Christ child they bowed down and

worshipped the newborn king. The Psalmist expressed it this way,
> *O come, let us worship and bow down, let us kneel before the Lord our Maker. O worship the Lord in the beauty of holiness; fear before him, all the earth.* Psalms 95:6; Psalm 96:9.

Paul declares,
> *Wherefore God also hath highly exalted him, and given him a name which is above every name: that at the name of Jesus every knee should bow, of things in heaven, and things in earth, and things under the earth; and that every tongue should confess that Jesus Christ is Lord, to the glory of God the Father.* Philippians 2:9-11.

Again, worship is integral to the lives of wise men and women. It is absolutely necessary for those who are on the journey initiated by God. But note, when we come to worship it is never to be entertained. The choir is not to perform but to lead us in worship. The preacher isn't there to entertain but to preach the unadulterated Word of God. We come not to be seen but to experience God's presence.

Worship requires that we come out of ourselves, this is especially true in the tradition of we people of African decent. Worship for African Americans is not only a celebration of our relationship with Christ but a celebration of the victories we've won both individually and collectively. Worship

> **Worship becomes the corporate expression of a people on a journey initiated by God. It is a collective expression of hope, faith and renewal.**

becomes the corporate expression of a people on a journey initiated by God. It is a collective expression of hope, faith and renewal.

Worship provides a context in which the African American community recalls it tragic and triumphal sojourn in a strange land. It is our confession that we believe we are passing through a strange land in anticipation of the promise land. Worship creates, for wise men and women who sojourn in a strange land, a system that cultivates and reinforces our sense of worth and helps us embrace and celebrate the God of our weary years and the God of our silent tears.

Carl R. Fielding, III in his article, *"African American Christian Worship,"* identifies three hallmarks of

African American Worship – celebration, invitation, and information. These hallmarks while providing entrée to God serve to preserve the nuances and manners of Black culture. Melvin Costen a former professor at ITC stated succinctly that we need to remind ourselves that Christian worship helps us establish solid belief systems in response to a culture and/or society that wishes to marginalize us.

Therefore, when we come to worship, we express our love and understanding of God in ways that accent the true meaning of life. It is in worship that everybody becomes somebody. We then celebrate not only the trials we've endured, the mountains we've climbed, and the obstacles we've overcome, but we celebrate the God who brought us through the agony and the ecstasy, through the terror and the tumult of the American Odyssey.

Worship for people of African descent becomes a unique cultural experience that allows the ethos of Afro-centricity to be experienced and highlighted throughout the worship experience. It is indeed a true celebration of both the hills and the valleys, the dark days and sunlit paths, the rain and sunshine, the friends and the enemies. But worship for us is also an invitation.

Worship for people of African descent was born of community. Therefore we always invite others to share in the caring fellowship of believers. Worship enables everyone who comes to participate and experience the total life of God through the church. This worship experience sends us into the world with a sense of belonging allowing us to make the greatest possible contribution to a needed world. But worship is incomplete if it does inform.

Worship, at its best, ought to challenge the believer spiritually and intellectually. Through preaching, teaching, music and witnessing the values of a community are shared. The information disseminated during worship ought to inspire, motivate, and prompt people to work for God. It ought to help the believer want to be transformed. It ought to tell the story of how we made it over. Worship, when filled with information, should give us a chance not only to learn about God, but learn about our own dynamics. The information about ourselves and about our possibilities should fill the worship experience, helping us believe that the journey of wise men and women is initiated by God and leads us to Christ who transforms us, and the culture around us.

Worship has also been an integral part of the African American tradition. Years ago, people came to church

> **Black people had to cultivate a forum where they could affirmed as people of worth, no matter what they did during the week, whether they were maids, janitors, garbage men, or street cleaners, they needed to know they were somebody.**

not just for worship but for affirmation. In a society that exploited, dehumanized, and devalued our ancestors, they needed a place to reinforce consistent clarification and affirmation of their inherent value to God and themselves.

Black people had to cultivate a forum where they could affirmed as people of worth, no matter what they did during the week, whether they were maids, janitors, garbage men, or street cleaners, they needed to know they were somebody. So on Sunday morning during the worship service, their nobodiness was transformed to somebodiness. They came to worship understanding that they were affirmed by God, and accepted by their brothers and sisters. Where they couldn't find freedom of expression in the larger society, church became the forum of complete and free expression. What humanity denied them during the week, God affirmed on Sunday morning.

The African American church still provides that forum and my admonition is that we place worship back at the center of our journey. Let your weeks begin and end with worship understanding like the wise men of the east that in worship you gave yourself completely to God.

The Wise men in the Christmas story bowed down and worshiped and then they gave their best; gold, myrrh, and frankincense. It is also in worship were learn to give our best to God and that is when God redirects our paths. The story ends by God informing the magi of Herod's evil intentions and instructing them to take a different route home. "And being warned of God in a dream that they should not return to Herod, they departed into their own country another way." Matthew 2:12.

Understand that worship is that place and that experience that allows you to become full enough to go the way God wants to direct you. That's why the writer of the Hebrews penned these potent words, "Not forsaking the assembling of ourselves together, as the manner of some is; but exhorting one another: so much the more, as ye see the day approaching." Hebrews 10:25.

Twin Towers, 74

Wise men and women have learned to worship and give themselves to God. They understand the journey is about God not them. Our fore-parents were well aware that God initiated the journey that's why they moved beyond the civil rights, beyond slavery and reconstruction, beyond their ancestors on the western coasts of Africa, and the Atlantic slave trade. They saw beyond Abraham, Ham, and Noah. They saw themselves in creation; sons and daughters of the true and living God. My prayer is that we wise men and women of the 21st century will, like our fore-parents, see beyond our present situations and see God as the initiator of our journey.

I hear the elders now, as they sing, "We've Come This Far By Faith". Yes we have. We have come this far by faith, leaning on the Lord, trusting in His Holy Word, He's never failed us yet

Twin Towers, 75

Spiritual Ears
For Social Change

Twin Towers, 76

Now the word of the Lord came to me saying, Before I formed you in the womb, I knew you and before you were born, I consecrated you. Then the Lord put forth his hand and touched my mouth and the Lord said to me, Behold I have put my words in your mouth; see, I have set you this day over nations and over kingdoms to pluck up and to break down, to destroy and to overthrow, to build and to plant. Jeremiah 1:4, 9.

> **This prophetic message trumpets a clarion call for change.**

This prophetic message trumpets a clarion call for change. Change is expressed in the graphic metaphoric language of the prophet's commission; pluck up, break down, destroy, build and planting. It was time for a change. Israel had forsaken God and now God had come to deal with their backsliding. It was time for a change. No, Israel wasn't ready for a change, but God sent a messenger with the message, "It's time for a change." While my message unlike Jeremiah's message wasn't forged out of any current crisis, I do believe, "It's time for a change".

It's time for a change, not because so much is out of order or because there are those who have not been faithful, but because I believe it's time for a change.

Neither am I a pessimist, thinking that the world is teetering and tottering on the brink of destruction or moving toward a day of annihilation, but I just believe it's time for a change. But we all know change always finds resistance. Isn't that true? All of us find ourselves resisting change.

I'm reminded of the movie "Malcolm X". Toward the end of the movie, the scriptwriter's focus on Malcolm's last day, the scene is moving and intense as Malcolm pensively stands reminiscing on his life, in the background Sam Cooke's song "Change Gon' Come" is playing,

> *"I was born by the river in a little tent,*
> *Oh and just like the river*
> *I been a runnin' ever since*
> *It's been a long, a long time coming but I know*
> *A change gon' come oh yes it will*
> *It's been too hard living but I'm afraid to die*
> *Cuz I don't know what's up there beyond the sky*
> *It's been a long, a long time coming but I know*
> *A change gon' come oh yes it will."*

Change is inevitable. But again change doesn't come without resistance. Even the greatest agent of change in all human history, Jesus Christ was faced with tremendous resistance. People didn't like Jesus because he represented change and they were not ready for change. But whether they wanted change or not, Jesus brought change. Jeremiah suggests in verse 10 that there is a need to do something different, that new times and new eras suggest doing things differently.

Jesus captured this same thought in Luke chapter 3 where he quotes from the book of Isaiah "Every valley shall be filled, and every mountain and hill shall be brought low; and the crooked shall be made straight, and the rough ways shall be made smooth. And all flesh shall see the salvation of God." Luke 3:5-6.

The point of departure is this, God expects us to be like Jesus. God has called us to be change agents, agents of transformation. This idea is based on my understanding of Genesis 1:27,28.

> *So God created man in his own image, in the image of God he created him; male and female created he them. And God blessed them, and God said unto them, Be fruitful, and multiply, and replenish the earth, and subdue it; and have dominion over the fish of the sea, and over the fowl of the air, and over every living thing that moveth upon the earth.*

> **Our problem though is that we don't want to take charge of the earth. We are content with just a little piece of the earth.**

This passage establishes humankind as leaders not reactors, as change agents not conformists. It's time for a change and I believe God is calling believers like us to lead out in the change.

Looking over our community and country, we need believers who will be become change agents. With growing unemployment, violence, drugs, immorality, and injustice, we need people who will be out front not only procreating but creating, multiplying, and subduing the earth, people who will control and take charge as commissioned by God from creation.

Our problem though is that we don't want to take charge of the earth. We are content with just a little piece of the earth. We have become satisfied with taking charge of our homes, our place where we work, and just a little nook carved out somewhere over the rainbow. But God said, that's not good enough, it's time for a change.

If God is going to come back for a church that is without a spot or a wrinkle, then someway, somehow

God's people must rise to the bigger responsibilities. God has created us in his image and after his likeness, and God is a big God; therefore we should trust God for big things, extraordinary things, things worthy of who we are as sons and daughters of God, members of the royal family of God, priests and kings of a higher order. It's time we change and we can make this change as God's chosen people.

Verses 1-3 suggest the context of this message. Jeremiah the young prophet, the son of Hilkiah the priest, began his prophetic ministry during the reign of the young king Josiah. The boy king Josiah, with encouragement from the young prophet Jeremiah, ordered the cleansing of the temple and subsequently discovered the old Law among the temple ruins. Josiah, after hearing the Law read, was convinced it was time for a change. The boy king and the young prophet instantly instituted a change. They called for a reconfiguring and a reconstruction of life in the kingdom.

That's how kingdom people respond. Jeremiah and Josiah led the march for change. I believe God is expecting the same of 21th century kingdom people. We are children of the Most High King and our God is capable of doing whatever He wants to do in and through us if we will let Him. Change is crucial now for our communities and country because for too long we have racked up the statistics, the statistics that inform us about what we can and cannot do.

For too long we have buried too many people prematurely; for too long we've made to many treks back and forth to graveyards, burying young children because of drugs or illicit lifestyles. For too long we have seen the erosion of family values with the consequence of broken lives and homes. For too long the church has witnessed this going out and coming in of people and behavior that demonstrates how far we've gone from God while we refuse to claim our rightful place as change agents of the kingdom. I do believe it's time for a change.

Let me allay your fears, I am optimistic. I have no doubts that we the people of God will rise to the occasion, but this is just a reminder; God doesn't want and neither can we afford benchwarmers and pew sitters. God wants everyone involved. Every believer must be a vibrant worker in the life of the church and in the life of the community. Kingdom people must make the drastic changes in their personal lives to become agents of change. Our lives must be the embodiment and model of the truth we say we believe. The church must take on the posture of being

God's elect and saying emphatically, in word and deed, God is doing a new thing and this new things requires change. It's time for a change!

> **It doesn't matter to some whether or not people in our communities can pay their bills.**

Verse ten of Jeremiah's chapter one declares that God wants to reconfigure and reconstruct community. But before God can bring about the drastic change needed in our communities there must be an internal reconfiguration and reconstruction of His people. Could it be that gentrification in our urban cities is a part of God's reconfiguration? Could this gentrification be the cause of the internal changes many Black churches in urban centers are experiencing? We people of color must understand that gentrification has no compassion. It does not care about Black people losing their homes and skyrocketing rental rates as property values rise.

It doesn't matter to some, whether or not people in our communities can pay their bills. It's time for a change and God will use what He wills to wake us up. God wants we people of African descent to rebuild our communities, to invest in our communities, but we won't until spiritual reconstruction has been done.

Here's why? We don't think we have any responsibility to the community any longer. We don't think the community is any of our concern since many of us no longer live in historically Black communities. While black churches are still located in the heart of the urban community, our hearts are often far removed. So we struggle now with what community really means.

Jesus provided an excellent example for the need of internal reconstruction in the 21st chapter of John's gospel. After the crucifixion of Christ, the discouraged disciples followed Peter back to their fishing boats. These were the men God had called to change the world. These were the men He commissioned to be fishers of men, but now they were back fishing for fish. They were in no condition to change the world. They needed reconstruction and Jesus knew it. On the shores of the Sea of Tiberius Jesus began the work of reconstructing these broken and discouraged disciples. He asked Peter, the soon to be reinstated leader, a probing question.

> "Simon, son of Jonas, lovest thou me more than these?" John 21:15.

Three times Jesus posed the same question to Peter. There was no doubt, Peter was listening to Jesus speak. He couldn't miss the missive of Christ. My contention is that in order for us to engage in positive and proactive change, in order to become agents of change, God must reconstruct us and reconstruction begins by hearing God speak. We must have spiritual ears. Verse four and five of Jeremiah one says.

> *"Now the word of the Lord came to me saying.,..."*

The text tells us that in order for change to take place, God's word must find us in the position that we can hear His word. Our ear must be attuned to His voice. We must have Spiritual Ears.

Now please understand, I am not advocating passively sitting in church taking copious pages of notes. I'm driving the point home that we must hear God's word in order to become agents of real change in our communities. Understand this, God's word convinces us that He has special work for us to do. This special work makes us different from those in the world. His Word makes us know that we are called to stand positively like trees planted by rivers of waters, unmovable and steadfast in His Word.

The wonder of God's word is that it comes to where we are. If we go about our daily activities with an ear toward heaven, our channels of communication and hearing not overridden with waves of worldly messages and signals, we will surely hear God. But as God speaks, we must posture ourselves to hear God. Spiritual ears know the difference between listening and hearing.

In Swahili, the word *"Unaskia"* helps us understand the difference between hearing and listening. *"Unaskia"* gives three connotations; to listen, to hear and to understand. This East African word moves hearing from merely receiving signals on the inner ear to moving words to the heart. It means hearing with the intent of understanding and responding.

So it must be for believers who plan to become change agents, we must tune our spiritual ears toward heaven letting the Word of God move past the outer ear to the inner ear and then to the heart. This is what Jesus meant on the beach that day, not many days after His resurrection, when he said to Peter,
> *"Simon, son of Jonas, lovest thou me more than these?" John 21:15.*

Peter responded,
> *"Lord, you know that I love you. "*

> **Are you really listening to hear what God has to say? Finding a place where there is little to no interference to the wavelengths of heaven, is the best opportunity to hear God speak.**

Jesus knew Peter was simply listening to Him, so He asked the question again, "Simon, son of Jonas, lovest thou me more than these?"

Peter replied again, "Lord, you know I love you."

When Jesus asked the third time, the Bible says that Peter was pricked in his heart. It was then Peter moved from listening to hearing. That's when his spiritual ears perched up and his listening became hearing and moved him to become one of the greatest change agents the world has ever known.

Are you really listening to hear what God has to say? Finding a place where there is little to no interference to the wavelengths of heaven, is the best opportunity to hear God speak.

In his book, <u>Upon this Rock</u>, Rev. Johnny Youngblood talks about his listening post. Early every morning, Rev. Youngblood rises before his family and goes into his library. There he sits in his favorite chair next to his favorite lamp and does nothing but listen for God. For thirty minutes he sits, no reading, no meditation, no talking, just listening. Can you hear God? Do you have a listening post? Do you understand God's call on your life? You've got to be willing and positioned to hear God speak to you individually as he speaks to all of us as a church. Change agents come by hearing God's voice.

But there are challenges to hearing God's word. There are interferences that effectively drown out God's voice. One of the greatest interferences is our inability to pull away from tradition. Tradition often bogs us down. Tradition has its place but often the pride of past achievements keeps us from pushing ahead to the new and the better. It keeps us from hearing God's voice for change. It keeps us from developing spiritual ears. The Apostle Paul wrote,
"How shall they hear without a preacher? And how shall they preach, except they be sent?" Romans 10:14,15.

Being sent here means hearing God's voice and acting on God's call. Like Jeremiah, we must be willing to take a different course; we must be willing to break from tradition. Jeremiah was born into a priestly family. His father Hilkiah was a priest. Everyone expected Jeremiah to follow in his father's footsteps and become a priest, but the Word of God says,

> *"Before I formed thee in the belly, I knew thee; and before thou camest forth out of the womb I sanctified thee, and I ordained thee a prophet to the nations." Jeremiah 1:5.*

God said in essence, "Your mamma and daddy may have been a priest, in fact your complete family lineage could have been priests, but I've called you to be a prophet to the nations."

How proud we are when we believe our children are going to follow in our footsteps. How many mothers and fathers have planned the entire life of their children? You told them what school they were going to attend, what career they would pursue, and even the type of person they should marry. But have you taught your children how to have spiritual ears? Have you allowed God to direct their lives?

I'll never forget how God changed the direction of my life. When I enlisted in the Navy in 1975, I had no plans of ever moving back to my hometown of Augusta, Georgia. I wanted to spread my wings and do my own thing. Atlanta was the place for me. So after a short stint in the Navy and an honorable discharge I made my way to the big city. I settled in to life in the big city.

But I soon found myself walking in my fathers footsteps by going to cosmetology school. My father and grandfather, Alfred Walker Sr. and Mark Walker, were barbers, so I accepted that as my heritage. Cosmetology was in the blood, so I thought. My family, while making a decent living, had never become rich in the trade, but this was in the early 80's when brothers and sisters were wearing geri-curls and I saw myself making a lot more money in the trade than they. In 1982 I moved back home to the city I thought I'd never return to with the thought of becoming a millionaire. My plan was to make a million dollars in three to five years doing geri-curls.

> But when I got back to Augusta God began to speak – right there in First Mt. Moriah Baptist Church, the church I grew up in.

But when I got back to Augusta God began to speak – right there in First Mt. Moriah Baptist Church, the church I grew up in, I thought I heard God's voice calling me to be a deacon like my father. My father had been the chairman of the Deacon's Ministry at First Mt. Moriah for 23 years. It seemed appropriate that his son would walk in his footsteps, so in 1982 I was ordained as a deacon at First Moriah Baptist Church. But in less than a year, I heard the voice of God say, "Your daddy's a deacon, but I didn't call you to be a deacon. There's nothing wrong with the office of a deacon. I love deacons and have a great work for deacons to do. But you have a higher calling. I'm calling you to preach."

It was time for a change in my life. It was time for a new direction.

The clarion call of Jeremiah's story is this; history doesn't determine the call of God on your life. It's what God has called you to do in life that matters. Everyone has a special calling, what we need to do is put on spiritual ears. Like Jeremiah, he has called us from the womb to pluck up, to root out, and to tear down, yet to build up and to plant. We are called to be change agent in our special calling and sphere of influence. As we put on spiritual ears, God will reconstruct us so that we can hear effectively His plan and our place in the plan for the reconfiguring and reconstruction of our communities.

Twin Towers, 91

Spiritual Tongues
for Social Change

> We must have spiritual utterance; a holy speech. We must have a dialogue that is set apart, a dialogue that is saturated with the sacred and grounded in righteousness.

Pondering again the need for change in our communities has brought me back to Jeremiah's prophetic words, "Then the Lord put forth His hand and touched my mouth, and the Lord said to me, 'Behold I have put My words in your mouth.'" Jeremiah 1:9.

Jeremiah's God-inspired words clue us to what must also take place in order for radical changes to happen in our communities, God's people must possess spiritual tongues. We must have spiritual utterance; a holy speech. We must have a dialogue that is set apart, a dialogue that is saturated with the sacred and grounded in righteousness. God must shape our communication in a way that it can reach the ears of God's people with maximum impact. This is what the text implies when it says,

"I have put My words in your mouth."

God is specific: not your words, the politician's words, or even the preacher's words, but My words. God's words must frame the dialogue for no human words can affect the kind of change needed in our communities.

God's word in your mouth! This powerful statement shows a dialogue between unequals; God's word, your mouth. The Creator speaking to the creature. What an awesome concept that God would condescend to form a partnership or covenant with us so that He can convey his words through these vessels of clay. Jeremiah received God's word in his mouth and just like Jeremiah, we too can receive God's word with as much validity, power, and legitimacy in ourmouths. Oh what a union, a partnership, what a covenant between unequals.

I'm reminded of Old Testament treaties/covenants. There were two types of treaties in the Old Testament; there was a Parity treaty that was negotiated between two equals. This was illustrated when two kings sat down to clarify borders and come to agreement about passing through each other's country.

Two equals worked out the agreement. Then there was the Suzerainty treaty. It was a treaty between unequals, between a larger and a lesser, a god and a human. This was the kind of treaty or covenant God made with Israel. It was between unequals, yet it was binding. And for spiritual Israel today, this is the covenant God makes with us when He says,

Twin Towers, 94

"I will put My word in your mouth."

God's word in your mouth. That's a huge concept. How in the world can we feel worthy to have the God of creation, the God of Israel, the God of all beginnings, Alpha and Omega, the first and the last, to deposit something as holy and as life-changing as His word in our little mouths. Who are we to say that we are legitimate carriers of God's word?

As amazing as this unthinkable undertaking is, God does this for His covenant people. So no matter what you think, no matter how little you feel, or how unworthy you think yourself to be, God wants to put his word in your mouth. Even more amazing, no matter how you have used your mouth in the past (foul, irreverent, and profane), God still will put His word in your mouth if you are willing to change.

This covenant God makes with us is critical for the radical changes needed in our community. Real change, substantive changes are made only when our speech, our utterances, what goes forth from our lips have real meaning and impact. Too often we spew words that are ineffectual, void of life-changing power. But God promises to put His life-changing word in our mouths, promises to make us His vehicles for carrying His word.

This is when we become His emissaries to reach other human beings that need God's transforming word. When God puts His word in our mouths, its like a mother helping a young child chew meat for the first time. While the child has teeth, it lacks experience and power to grind the meat well enough to eat it.

> **People put their words in God's mouth when they misrepresent or misquote God's word.**

Therefore the mother takes a small piece of the meat and chews it until it is fit for the child to eat. In the same way God knows the world is not prepared to receive His word, it is strong meat, so He puts the word in our mouths allowing us to chew on it until it is fit for the world to receive.

This is what the covenant is about. It is about bringing God's word to a world that desperately needs agents of change. The word of God is a response to both our own inadequacies and the inadequacies of the world. His words, not our own, nor the erroneous words that fill so much of our air ways today, but God's indisputable word is needed to bring substantive change to a sick world.

But the challenge for today is that there are many who are flipping the script, they are altering God's word, they are putting their word in God's mouth. How are they altering God's word? I'm glad you asked. The script is flipped when you share your words with the pretense you are sharing God's word. You put words, your words in God's mouth when you change or misappropriate God's word. When you quote what you purport to be in the Bible and on examination it isn't there, you are putting your words in God's mouth. Like the gentlemen I overheard trying to impress a friend with is biblical scholarship, saying, "the Bible says, 'God bless the child who's got his own.'"

While that may sound biblical, I hope we all know that's not biblical – that's the blues. People put their words in God's mouth when they misrepresent or misquote God's word. These are the tongues of the immature.

God is calling for spiritual tongues, tongues that have been touched by tongs from the altar of God, tongues that have received the life-changing words of God. Oh what power the church would have if all of God's people resolved within their hearts to make sure God's word were an active part of their vocabulary. What changes would happen in our communities if

the word of God were a part of our daily lives and were rooted deep in our hearts? It would in effect be like John's expression about the coming Messiah,
> *"the word became flesh and dwelt among us."*
> *John 1:14.*

What a powerful statement. When God puts His word in our mouths His word comes alive in us and brings change in our communities. We dare not change God's word. Just like the offensive coach on a football team. The offensive coach has been given latitude to call the plays. The head coach watches while the offensive coach sends in play after play. But then the head coach decides that he will call the next play. No matter what the offensive coach thinks, the head coach has put his words in his mouth and he dare not change it. And no matter what we think, no matter how we feel, we cannot change God's word. His word and his word alone must be in our mouths. He is the head coach!

There is still another challenge – that of speaking the word once God has put it in our mouths. There is no natural overflow of the word once it is imparted. We must speak the word. There must be an intentional effort to share the word with others. It is dangerous to have the word of God in our mouths and for whatever reason, we don't speak it. The dangers lie in the fact that our words are life or death to others. When we don't speak the word of God to our families and our communities we are denying them life. When God puts words in our mouths we must share it.

Lives are depending on the life-changing words of God. But often our fear of sharing the word comes because we have not heard the word ourselves. God has put the words in our mouth but the words have never gotten to our ears. Whatever your calling may be, whether it be a minister, evangelist, a doorkeeper, a deacon, if your life doesn't suggest that you are carrying the word, I implore you to hear God's word.

Paul was adamant about living the word because he didn't see the value of preaching to others while missing the boat himself. Please don't have the word of God in your mouth and don't hear it for yourself. Let God's word impact your life. If there is going to be change in our communities God's people must be in position to hear God's word so that we can share His word. Once the church positions itself to be emissaries for God, I believe change will come; radical change in our school systems, local governments and national governments.

Jeremiah was youthful and inexperienced, but God called him and put His words in his mouth and brought change to the nation. God will do the same for His church if we will ready ourselves and avail ourselves of His word. We will become agents of change irrespective of our lot in life. The single parent, God will use. The corporative executive, God will use. The physician or clinician, God will use. God will put a word in your mouth even though you are aged and your steps may be few and feeble, or you're living on a fixed income, or you're new to the community. It doesn't matter, God will use any one whose willing to be used. It's not the vessel that brings the change but the word of God. God's word, believe it or not, is the only real agent of change. This was graphically illustrated in the ministry of Jesus.

There was a young man by the name of Legion who lived among the tombs. Day and night he, howled scourging and cutting himself. No one could tame him. Jesus went across to Sea of Geneseret to meet him. After an interchange with Jesus, after a dialogue with the Messiah, Jesus cast out the demons, and the scripture says,
> *"He sat at the feet of Jesus clothed and in his right mind." Mark 2:25.*

The word of God can change even the worst

> We can no longer afford a kind of sanctimonious lip service that does nothing more than stir the pot. It's time for spiritual tongues that can speak life to the valley of dry bones.

situations. If we will allow ourselves to be changed by God's word, then God will use us to change others.

But change will only take place when everyone gets on board. The lazy folks must get up; the sleeping folks must wake up; the gossiping folks must shut up; the dishonest folks must confess up; the estranged and separated folks must make up; the disgusted must sweeten up; the lukewarm must get fired up; the dry bones must be shaken up; the leading folks must live up; the folks who owe the church must pay up; and the real soldiers of Christ must stand up. This will happen as God puts His word in our mouths.

Change is long overdue. It's time for us to speak life to our communities. We can no longer afford a kind of sanctimonious lip service that does nothing more than stir the pot. It's time for spiritual tongues that can speak life to the valley of dry bones. There are many people in our communities that have no other help but us. They are on their last leg of life, they see no other way out, we are their only hope. We've got to let them know that change is real and possible. We must speak the word that God has put in our mouths to affect change in theirs. Will you be a spiritual tongue to speak life into our communities?

Twin Towers, 102

Notes

Pharaoh Meets Great Jehovah
Part I

Reflecting on our pilgrimage as African Americans from slavery to freedom, I believe we become confused at times about our roles. Facing contemporary Pharaohs that continue to push us from the center to the margins, we often question just what role God would have us play in bringing change to our communities. Our lot is much like Moses.

> **Facing contemporary Pharaohs that continue to push us from the center to the margins, we often question just what role God would have us play in bringing change to our communities.**

"And God spoke unto Moses and said unto him, I am the Lord. And I appeared unto Abraham and Isaac, and unto Jacob by the name of God Almighty, but by my name Jehovah was I not known to them. Go in, tell Pharaoh king of Egypt to let the children of Israel go out of his land." Exodus 6:2,3,11.

Our text finds Moses being sent by God to confront Pharaoh. The message of Moses was simple, "Let my people go!"

God was ready now to deliver the family of Jacob, the

progenitor of the chosen people of God from Egyptian bondage. This was the final months of Israel's long saga in Egypt, specifically the whole period of servitude and bondage. Israel's pilgrimage to Egypt was prompted by a famine in their home country. Providentially, God sent Joseph, the son of Jacob ahead in an unusual way (sold into Egyptian slavery by his own brothers), to preserve this chosen family.

Joseph, a Hebrew slave, miraculously became prime minister of Egypt commissioned with the special task of handling famine relief. After hearing about the famine relief program in Egypt, Jacob sent his sons to Egypt to purchase food. While there, Jacob's sons meet their forgotten brother Joseph, who subsequently sends for the entire family to come to Egypt.

The biblical script informs us that seventy went down to Egypt with Jacob. But after years of the favor of God, seventy turned to over a million Israelites. This family who had been welcome, now was feared. The Bible says that there rose a Pharaoh that knew not Joseph. The chosen people of God no longer had protection in the palace. They went from being favored guests to servants and then to slaves. How can you be a change agent when you are the oppressed?

Our text finds Moses still staggering under the great

theophany experienced at the burning bush. He stepped into the presence of this holy and awesome God and was commissioned to return to the land from whence he had fled 40 years earlier. God was sending him back to be the catalyst, the re-presentation of God in a land where God's people had been captured, castigated, and marginalized. Moses would now be the instrument of liberation for his people. But Moses was confused about his role. He just couldn't see how God could use him to be the liberator. So He argued and debated with God until he finally accepted the mantle of responsibility. His assignment, tell Pharaoh, "to let my people go."

The task would not be easy for God warned Moses that Pharaoh would not receive the message. God's Word to Moses,
>"*I will harden Pharaoh's heart.*" Exodus 4:21.

But something interesting happened when Moses confronted Pharaoh. Not only did Pharaoh refuse to let the people of God go, he increased their work. Pharaoh response might have gone like this, "Oh, so you people don't have enough work to do. I can solve that!" Then Pharaoh changed the rules. He required them to make the same amount of bricks but now they must supply their own straw. How cruel. But when

Pharaoh doesn't know Joseph or Joseph's God what more could be expected. The people then complained to Moses and Aaron, "look what you two have done. You've made Pharaoh angry and he has increased our work." Moses went to God with this question,

> *"And Moses returned unto the Lord and said, Lord, wherefore hath thou so evil entreated this people; why so is it that you sent me?*

Moses asked two pressing questions; Why have you treated us so harshly? Why did you really send me?

The issue and problem of the text is one of role confusion. It didn't work our like Moses thought it should have, so he was in a quandary about his role. Confusion sets in about our role in a matter when we don't understand the way things are going. We sometimes question whether or not God has sent us as emissaries when the mission is not clear. We become concerned about our calling when we aren't able to calculate the time of our liberation.

We often define our role based on our ability to dictate the timetable. And when we can't pin down the time, we raise questions that have no validity? We ask, why? Why this? Why that? Why didn't it happen the way I had it plan? Let me share something with you, the Bible isn't a "why" book, and God isn't

> In the church, as much as we might not like to admit it, God uses us, frail human beings, to build His kingdom.

under obligation to answer any questions. Take a look in the Bible, you will discover as I have, that there are plenty "whys" asked, but they are never answered by God. Understand, you can rise all the "whys" you want, that doesn't mean God will give you an answer. The question,

"Why do the heathen rage?"– no answer. Psalm 2:22.

"Why doth thou stand afar off?"–no answer. Psalm 10:30.

Even Jesus on the Cross asked, "Why hast thou forsaken me?" – no answer. Matthew 23:25.

From Genesis to Revelation we see the consistent thread of God acting, but not always answering.

We see in Moses' response to confronting Pharaoh the human problem of role confusion. In the church, as much as we might not like to admit it, God uses us, frail human beings, to build His kingdom. Like Moses, we have misgivings about our roles when we are called to confront difficult situations. We have romanticized scripture so much that we have taken the edge off the idea of the call of God. It is now glamorized and popularized where ministry is more about feeling good than being obedient.

It isn't always about how good you feel and how good you look when it comes to God. When you are called to confront Pharaoh, it's not about you. We must never confuse our roles with who calls us, who sanctions us, who sends us. If Moses has just remembered who called him and God's warning, "I will harden Pharaoh's heart," he would have realized it wasn't about him. God was moving to build His kingdom.

I'm fearful about what I'm hearing in this age of romanticized ministry. The constant buzz about "anointing." "Make sure you have the anointing!" "The anointing is on me" all sound like sounding brass and tinkling symbols. This kind of talk treats the anointing, the Spirit of God, as if it were a toy. It seems that everyone wants to be caught up in the Spirit. The talk is often about what is appropriate and what's popular as a "Word Church."

I am interested in both the Word and the Anointing, but know that the Word is not a toy and the Anointing is not a game. The serious business of being filled with the Spirit of God challenges us to live the Word. God isn't interested in how much we can recall scripture; God isn't interested in how much grey matter we have; He's not interested in establishing a "Talented Tenth"; He's not interested in where you went to school. God's only concern is whether or not He can use you.

God arranged the whole scene so that Pharaoh might meet the Great Jehovah. Understanding the sovereignty of God, we come to understand that history is never about the oppressor or the opposition. Scripture reveals that there is nothing too hard for God and there is no Pharaoh too big for God to handle. God sent Moses to fulfill the covenant He made with Abraham, Isaac, and Jacob. There was no need for Moses to have fear about the task or questions about His role. God's words to Moses were intended to do two things; first to give comfort.

> *"I appeared unto Abraham and Isaac and Jacob as the God Almighty, but by my name Jehovah was I not known."*

It wasn't that Israel didn't know the name Jehovah, they were familiar with the name but not the person. They had known God as El Shaddai, God Almighty, the God of power. The creation story in Genesis chapter one reveals God as creator. He is Elohim, who speaks into existence everything from nothing.

"He spoke and it was done. He commanded and it stood fast."

God is first known in his power, but when He spoke to Moses, He revealed himself in His being. God says, "I am the Lord God."

He reveals Himself as the great "I Am". God says in essence, "I am the one who created and I am the one who sustains. I am the one who calls, sanctions, supports, sustains and nurtures. I Am that I Am. Nothing has changed Moses, you can trust me." What a powerful word of encouragement for those who are sent as emissaries.

When you are confronted by the Pharaohs of the world and feel confused about your role, take comfort in knowing that God is a God of being. The great epic movie "Roots" reminds me again of this Great Jehovah, this God who intervenes in the plight of humankind. It was Jehovah God who protected our forefathers from the western coast of Africa all the way through slavery. It was the great "I Am" that guided people of African descent through the civil rights struggle.

Some would like to forget about our struggle. But remembering the struggle helps us to remember our role and our God. It helps us remember that God is not just powerful–He is personal. God declares, "I Am." We can take comfort in knowing God's name and Who He is.

> **The success of the Moses' mission was not guesswork. God had promised the land to His chosen people; Moses' job was simply to remind Israel about the promise.**

Finally, God's message to Moses was assurance for the role he was called to play. The scripture records,

"I have also established my covenant with them, to give them the land of Canaan, the land of their pilgrimage wherein they were strangers." Exodus 4:3.

The success of the Moses' mission was not guesswork. God had promised the land to His chosen people; Moses' job was simply to remind Israel about the promise. The promise was made in the form of a binding covenant. God instructed Abraham,

"I will make you into a great nation and I will bless you; I will make your name great and you will be blessing. I will bless those who

bless you, and whoever curses you I will curse; and all peoples on earth will be blessed through you." Genesis 12:2,3.

Pharaoh was to meet the Great Jehovah because God made a covenant that He would not renege on. The covenant was Moses assurance about his role in God's plan for Israel's redemption. You've got to know that God guarantees your freedom and the guarantee is through the covenant. Moses could stand before Pharaoh with confidence because his role was guaranteed by the covenant God made with Abraham.

Often God uses others to help bring about his purpose. We must be clear on the issue of what our roles are as the elect of God. We must not be ashamed. We must not compromise the role God has given us. We must stand when all else seems to fail. We must stand on God's word and be the light to the nation we've been called to be. We have been called to be change agents.

We have been called to help Pharaoh meet Great Jehovah for change in our communities. Don't let modern day Pharaohs frighten you about your role. God "ain't" afraid of Pharaohs and neither should you be. You can know what God wants you to be and where he wants you to be, but you must be assured of God's name, take comfort in who God is, and be confident in the reality of the covenant. God established the covenant; therefore He is bound to bring it to fruition. You can take that to the bank.

Be convinced, as I am, that it's time to tell Pharaoh, "Let my people go." God established His covenant in order to secure His people. He's stood watch long enough. He's ready now to bring change to our communities and this country. Step into your role. Be willing to stand and go against the odds. Let Pharaoh meet the Great Jehovah. If you are willing to abide in Him and know who He is and understand that he secured the covenant at Calvary, then God will use you to transform not only the community you live in, but also your city, and this country. Remember, God is faithful to His word. His covenant is an eternal covenant. You can count on God because He is the same yesterday, today, and forevermore.

Pharaoh Meets Great Jehovah
Part II

The story of the Exodus provides an excellent backdrop for understanding the plight of we people of African descent. In the previous message we discovered that it was God's purpose that Pharaoh meet Great Jehovah. God wanted Pharaoh to know who He was, but He wanted Israel also to understand that they were His agents of change. He wanted to use Israel as a representative of Him and the kingdom; not just to be a light to themselves.

> We think because God has sent us on the important mission of confronting Pharaoh and He has used us to represent or re-present Him to the world that our timetable ought to be His timetable.

It's easy to become a light to yourself, to confuse or misappropriate your purpose and role in life as mentioned in the previous sermon. Moses became quickly undone when God's time didn't correspond to his own. When Pharaoh delayed in releasing God's people Moses became confused about his role. And we often do the same thing.

We think because God has sent us on the important mission of confronting Pharaoh and He has used us to represent or re-present Him to the world that our timetable ought to be His timetable. We confuse our roles and we begin to think everything is predicated upon us, and our understanding and perception. This finds us trying to play God's role. But we can't confuse our roles with the role of God.

God wants to use us, but not as an end to ourselves for that will lead us as African Edenic people to take on the role of the oppressor and start being towards our brothers what the oppressor has been towards us. Because we've been blessed a little now, we've confused our roles and we think we are God; we think we have the answers. That's one of the reasons we see community the way it is.

Too many of us have been so blessed we don't know God still wants to use us to help others. We think the blessing stops with us. That's why we have folk in the church and pastors around this country always talking about being blessed. "I'm blessed," is the new catch phrase. The prayer and the spiritual mantra of many is "bless me and my wife, my son, my daughter, us four and no more. Amen."

God doesn't bless us to hoard it. The gospel writer Luke tells the story of the farmer who had planted

well and had brought in a bumper crop. He had more than enough. In fact so much that he said,
> *This is what I will do. I will tear down my barns and build bigger ones, and there I will store all my grain and my goods. And I will say to myself, "You have plenty of good things laid up for many years. Take life easy; eat, drink, and be merry.* Luke 12:18,19.

The Lord visited him that night, and said, "You fool! This very night your life will be demanded from you. Then who will get what you have prepared for yourself." Luke 12:20.

The scripture empathetically states, God doesn't bless us to hoard the blessings. It behooves us and becomes more apparent to me that this parable is speaking to this age. God wants us to know the blessing is not just an icon, but it is included in the plan–God's plan of salvation and liberation for his entire people. I really believe we're going to get it right as we look back on those great African American giants who trod the path before us. Those who came and gave all they had not seeking an end for themselves or in themselves. Those now numbered among that "great cloud of witnesses".

Often in spite of ourselves God has used us and the contributions we have made to our community and country as a witness that we are an absolutely blessed people. We are regal and prominent in so many ways and by virtue of God's blessings, pronouncements, and presence in our lives. Like ancient Israel, we have seen the best and worst of times. We have always been dual in our deportment. We've always had to know both cultures. We learned early the majority language (The King's English) but we have always stayed fluent in our own cultural dialect.

Never entertain the notion that our children can't learn the King's English. We are still in Egypt and our children still must understand that we maybe liberated physically but there are still Pharaoh's in the land. That's what the Word of God comes today to remind us of.

> *"And I have heard the groaning of the children of Israel whom the Egyptians keep in bondage, and I have remembered my covenant."* (Exodus 6:5.)

We've got to know we still have much against us. There are still cries of inequality and injustice coming from our communities. God's message to Moses is applicable to us, "And I have heard the groaning of the children of Israel."

We must take comfort in knowing God does fulfill His promise. He made a covenant with Abraham, Isaac, and Jacob and He was fulfilling it through Moses. God said to Moses, "I have heard the groaning."

God said in other words Israel, I am familiar with, I am inundated with, I am knowledgeable of what's going on in your daily lives. And what was going on? It was the promotion of Pharaoh's kingdom to the demise of the Hebrew slaves. Pharaoh's sinister plot to break the backs of God's people is seen as he tasked them doubly. Read the biblical script. Pharaoh told them to do the same amount of labor as before but this time without straw. In the effort to meet production, Israel was dispersed throughout the kingdom gathering stubble. Pharaoh not only didn't help them with straw, he withheld the straw.

> **When it comes down to who God is and his promises, oftentimes our hearts become faint, our heads become nauseous with the feeling that we've been rejected because the promise doesn't come as soon as we expected it.**

When your world is falling apart, it's hard to believe that God's promise is still in force. When it comes down to who God is and his promises, oftentimes our hearts become faint, our heads become nauseous with the feeling that we've been rejected because the promise doesn't come as soon as we expected it. Sometimes when your burdens are increased and you feel that they are too much to bear, when you are up against it and your back is against the wall, and you don't know which way to turn, you feel abandoned; you feel that the same God who promised you has now abdicated his responsibility.

You feel left alone on your own Isle of Patmos. You feel like nobody understands, like you don't have anyone to turn to. You feel the same rejection Israel must have felt has they scowled the kingdom for straw, that feeling that drove them to cry out to Moses and Aaron believing these two leaders had messed things up for them.

They were in servitude, but at least the master provided them straw. Moses went back to the Lord confused saying in my paraphrase version, "what have you done and why have you treated the people this way and why have you really sent me. You told me you would send me with a message that would free the people. But look at what Pharaoh has done."

Often times when God's timing is not our timing, we become confused about the promise, the promise of deliverance that doesn't come in a timely fashion. "Where is your God now," the nay-sayers ask. "What is your religion doing now," retort the envious watchers. Why do you keep on going down to that church now that things aren't going the way you said they would go? What about your faith in God? What happens when the straw is removed?

The removal of the straw by Pharaoh I believe parallels what has taken place in America in recent years. America has taken back the straw given over forty years ago. We had the Voting Rights Act of 1964, the Civil Rights Act of 1965, but now over the past dozen or more years we've seen the withdrawal of the straw and the retarding of the clock. There has been more legislation introduced to turn back the clock of equity than ever before. We've witnessed the redistricting of lines that were drawn in all probability to make things fair and to make things equitable in life, but now over the past dozen or more years the Pharaohs of the land have redrawn the district lines with one apparent purpose in mind, to reinstate the role of superiority.

America has taken back the straw. No more praying in schools and no more allocating of time for religious purposes, unless it's given in the way pleasing to the government. It just appears to me, America has taken back the straw. But Pharaoh's action doesn't startle or surprise me because I believe the Lord has allowed this to happen as He did with Israel in order that Pharaoh will one day meet the Great Jehovah.

So I don't become overly concerned with what Pharaoh does, whether Pharaoh has a seat in the White House, the State House, or the City House. These Pharaohs only occupy an earthly throne. Isaiah put it all in perspective when he describes the Lord sitting above the circle of the earth. Thank God, there is another throne with another King sitting on it. Pharaoh and all other earthly kings will one day have to meet Him. So don't become undone when we witness Pharaoh's straw tactics. God is setting it up for Pharaoh to meet Him.

He is setting it up so that all those who oppose His kingdom might come to know who He is. We just need to be patient. He will deliver His promises, but in the interim, while we're waiting there is a work for us to do. The waiting God calls us to is not passive. God's waiting is an assertive, aggressive waiting. It is a call to stand up and stand against. We must be willing to confront Pharaoh whether the vicissitudes

> We hear a lot of talk about Black men being irresponsible, and there are some irresponsible Black men, but they are no more irresponsible than other men.

of life or local, state, or federal governments that have proactive plans that oppose the kingdom of God.

Understand God has a purpose and God has a plan. The existence of churches in this community and the existence of African Americans in this country is proof of God's purpose and plan. God planted this church and our people from the very foundation of the world therefore we need not worry about being in jeopardy of becoming extinct. No matter what you think or what Pharaoh does, the Black Church nor the Black man will be absent from the American landscape.

We hear a lot of talk about Black men being irresponsible, and there are some irresponsible Black men, but they are no more irresponsible than other men. The talk about irresponsibility among Black men is to heighten the hype about the annihilation of our Black boys, but we need not worry – these are still God's children. God's church, God's people. God's men and women are not in jeopardy of becoming extinct.

The prophetic voice cries out, "I've called you from your mother's womb. I've blessed you so that you can become a blessing, not to be lamp or a light to yourself. Don't be confused about your role."

Our role is to be lights to the nation. And because God has commissioned us with the light that can't be extinguished, the most important thing for the Black Church to remember is not to become undone by oppressive forces but to know that we are still God's agents of love and reconciliation in this world. We are sent with a salvific message and methodology that is adaptable. We must understand that our methods must match the different times and the circumstances under which we live. 20th century methods will not work with 21th century people.

In order to communicate effectively God's message to the new urban dwellers and new Pharaohs, we must understand the times. These times can be so confusing. We must take advantage of the time. We must seize this opportunity to educate our children and ourselves to a bigger and broader world view.

Many of our youth aren't able to discern what is oppressive and unrighteous; they move into the world with defective lenses that make it difficult and sometime impossible to detect where people of African descent stand in this country. Our youth need to understand that Pharaoh still controls corporate America and the academic institutions regardless of what they may think or experience.

That's why it's important to seize the time. Don't be fooled about the land or the landscape of those who occupy seats of power. In spite of what Pharaoh does to retard the clock and take away the straw, we can take comfort in God's word. He promised that He would be with us. He is the one who commissioned us. And He will be the one who sustains and protects us. Over four hundred years we've been in a country that has despised us, yet we still helped to build this land of ours into the greatest country in the world. No one can nay-say the fact that God has been with us.

I'm so glad we don't have to become undone. We can rest assured that God has called us and wants us to share the salvific word with one another, a lost generation and a lost world. God's purpose is that ultimately Pharaoh will meet Him. We must be a church willing to establish God's covenant and God's word, both here and in our communities. We need to be willing to not only sponsor but help our young people and others who want to serve in public offices.

We need children of the Most High to take a seat along side Pharaoh. We need those who are retired from class roms and corporate America to run for public office. We need God's people in this land and all over the land. God commands,
> *"Be fruitful and multiply and subdue the earth."* Genesis 1:26.

God has a plan and it is to share salvation to the ends of the earth. The Black Church has been instrumental for hundreds of years in spreading God's message, but God isn't through with us or any of His people yet. There is still work to be done. There are still Pharaohs to confront and God doesn't want us to become undone. The song writer said it so well, "Time is filled with swift transitions, naught on earth unmoved can stand, build your hopes on things eternal; hold on to God's unchanging hand."

Believe God for the impossible. Believe that God is real. Hold on to God's hand no matter how bleak it looks, no matter how confused and compromised you may seem. Don't you ever give up on God! He promised He would deliver us. We just need to believe and patiently wait.

Remember, God's timing is always right. Paul writes,
> *"In the fullness of time, God sent forth His son."* Galatians 4:4.

> **The first liberation was from the bondage of sin. Therefore, we need not worry about Pharaoh or any enemy.**

John follows with this promise,
> *"God so loved the world that He gave His only Son."* John 3:16.

The first liberation was from the bondage of sin. Therefore, we need not worry about Pharaoh or any enemy. The story is told of a young girl who one day went for a ride with her father. It was a warm day and since the air-conditioning in the car didn't work, they were forced to let down the windows. Driving down a dusty country road, a bee flew in the car. The little girl panicked. The father quickly accessed the situation, grabbed the bee in his hand, held it for a moment, and then let it go. In the process of protecting his daughter, the father took the sting of the bee. The little girl looked bewilderedly at her father and said, "Daddy, your hand is red, the bee stung you."

The father replied with a look of love, "It's okay baby, you don't have to worry now, bees only have one sting."

We don't have to worry now. God sent His son in the fullness of time to protect us from the sting. At Calvary Christ endured the sting for us. Paul writes to the church of Corinth,
> *Death has been swallowed up in victory. Where, O death is your victory? Where, O death is your sting? The sting of death is sin, and the power of sin is the law. But thanks be to God. He gives us the victory though our Lord Jesus Christ. Therefore, my dear brothers, stand firm. Let nothing move you. Always give yourselves fully to the work of the Lord, because you know that our labor in the lord is not in vain.* 1 Corinthians 15:54-58.

God's has come down to help us to be who we are. Hold on to His hand. I don't care what comes. Hold to His hand. No matter what comes. You hold on. Dark and dreary day, long and toilsome nights– hold on to His hand. Move valleys than hills–hold to His hand. More rain than sunshine–hold to His hand. More disappointments than celebrations–hold to His hand. God will ultimately vindicate all of us. We just need to hold on to His unchanging Hand.

Twin Towers, 130

Notes

Pharaoh Meets Great Jehovah
Part III

> We are a very blessed people, but our blessings are because of God and not because of us. The truth be told, God blesses us in spite of ourselves.

Our text for consideration continues the study of the Exodus experience discussed in the previous messages. I want to use as a point of departure the following verse,

Wherefore say unto the children of Israel, I am the Lord and I will bring you out from under the burdens of the Egyptians, and I will rid you out of their bondage. And I will redeem you with a stretched out arm and with great judgments.

Today is a wonderful time to be alive. This period, this epoch for many of us as Christians and more particularly as African American Christians, is a wonderful time. We are a very blessed people, but our blessings are because of God and not because of us. The truth be told, God blesses us in spite of ourselves.

That's why it's so difficult for me to buy into and invest in the prosperity gospel that is so prevalent today. It appears more brag than blessing. It is as if God is somehow manipulated to bless only a special few.

My understanding from God's word is that the blessings of God are never an end in themselves. The blessings are just symbols of God's real blessing, the blessing to be His and for Him to be ours. The blessing is the privilege of being in relationship with the Almighty God. The blessing is in the essence of being, not in the thing that comes as a result of our being. And so the time we live in is wonderful simply because we are living in it and we belong to God, not because of what we have.

This is important to understand because many among us are still making brick without straw, many are facing difficulties. Take heart. God never wants us to become undone by our circumstances. Take comfort. God's ultimate plan will come to fruition. We are working out our own salvation on the heels of hundreds of years of ancestry. We are working out our own understanding of who God is, what God does for us and how He promotes us on the hinges of African American patriarchs and matriarchs. God has an ultimate plan.

That's why we should never become undone by outward appearances and/or circumstances. In order to be God's people, we must focus on God or else we will misappropriate not only His words but we will misconstrue the message. God's desire is to deliver us from bondage.

Our problem is that many don't believe we are in bondage. Many of us would not claim that we are undone by daily events, but a close examination might prove otherwise. Pharaoh has had an effect on us. It's one thing to be a Pharaoh, it's another thing to be influenced by Pharaoh so that you take on Pharaoh-tic persuasion.

The word Pharoah-tic is not in Webster's Dictionary -- that's my word. I've called it into being. What I mean by Pharoah-tic is to become like Pharaoh. One of the great travesties that we have witnessed over the past fifty years is so many of our brothers and sisters who have invested in taking on Pharaoh-tic characteristics. So many have wanted to be like Pharaoh; we all, truth being told, have acquiesced in some ways to becoming like Pharaoh.

We can no longer masquerade as if everything is all right. Our communities are experiencing the pain of so many who have taken on Pharaoh's ways. We see it at election time. How is it that we people of African descent who have traversed the stony path and endured such ill treatment, could acquiesce so easily because of power. Everyone wants some power, but at what cost?

One day you see brothers and sisters standing, dancing and praising in the court of God. The church is filled with accolades and attributions to God one day and the next day you see the same brothers and sisters standing with Pharaoh–being Pharaoh-tic.

The Pharoah-ticing that often fills our communities can cause us to become undone, especially when you see folks who aren't brave enough to come out and say what they believe or what they are. But take comfort, Pharaoh will meet the Great Jehovah. As I mentioned in the previous messages, we can take comfort in God's name. God declares, I am God. I am Elohim. I am Yahweh. I am El Shaddai. I am Jehovah God.

So don't be undone by the vicissitudes of life. Don't vacillate between what's righteous and what's unrighteous. Know that God is God. But we can take added comfort in God's covenant. The covenant is the pact God made with Abraham, Isaac, and Jacob. It's God's promise of deliverance that is guaranteed by His name. "Through many dangers, toils and snares, We have already come."

No we didn't get where we are on flowery beds of ease. "We've come this far faith, leaning on the Lord, trusting in His holy word."

> **God heard our cry. He is a God of compassion. He knows how much we can bear.**

In our distress, we were reminded in the previous message, God heard our cry. He is a God of compassion. He knows how much we can bear. God does not intend for us to be unduly treated or mistreated. He will allow so much to go on, then, He will come to see about us.

You don't have to live to be a centenarian, a person who has experienced one hundred years, to know that God does what he says. All of us experience times when we believe God is somewhere in the distance, beyond the dim unknown, but somehow, someway, miraculously, God keeps His promise and comes to see about us. That's the God resolve we discover in our text. God declares to Moses and to us. "I will bring you out from under the burdens of the Egyptians."

We can take comfort in the resolve of God.

There is a resolution and a resolve that God has to ensure true liberation. No, we don't wear manacles;

no, we are not behind bars, yet there is a systemic oppression that we face from day-to-day called racism. We are not called to play the race card every time there is something done wrong. Sometimes God intends for us to suffer through knowing and believing He is in control. Don't worry about Pharaoh or those with Pharaoh-tic spirits or who want to be Pharaoh. God will deliver.

Take comfort in His resolve. God says He will deliver us and that's what we must believe. I think we all understand by now, that no matter how much we want to make things equal, no matter how much we hope for the playing field to be level, there will always be those who are willing to take a few dollars to keep things the way they've always been. But I love the way the story in Exodus ends. After repeated confrontations and repeated refusal by Pharaoh, God moved to His final resolve.

At times God will suspend his grace to someone and still demand obedience as He did with Pharaoh. Six times Moses demanded, under the direction of God, that Pharaoh let God's people go. But in the ninth chapter of Exodus verse 14 through 16 God brings the drama to a close. He tells Moses to stand aside and watch me work. Moses repeats the command for the seventh time, Pharaoh again hardens his heart and refuses to obey God's command. The quiver of God's arrows of wrath are now unleashed.

God had given Pharaoh chance upon chance, but now there was no more respite from the wrath of God. Pharaoh must meet Great Jehovah. Take comfort in God's resolve. He will come and change life and make life palatable for us.

And know this, God's does have an ultimate plan and it's bigger than we are, in fact it's bigger than what we can imagine. Look at how brilliant we are. Look at how fascinating we are. Look at how the world sees us and is fascinated with our ebony hue, we sons and daughters of Africa. Look at how they are fascinated at just the way we are. Isn't it interesting, everybody wants to be like us?

Everybody wants to put a bounce in their step. Everybody wants to speak our dialect and use our vernacular. It appears that now everyone in the world wants to be included as a minority. Everybody wants to say they too have a dream. Everybody wants to be included as the downtrodden. Everybody wants freedom from Pharaoh's bondage. But God's ultimate plan transcends Pharaoh's bondage.

You see, Moses, like we so often do, missed the big dream, the big picture. Moses thought the plan was the exodus, but God's plan was redemption. Oh, what would it be like if Moses were our god; where would we be now had Moses had his way? God's ultimate plan was for Israel to be redeemed and liberated to worship and serve Him. The text spells it out, "I will redeem you with a stretched out arm and with great judgments; I will redeem you."

That's the purpose of God's grace and that is His purpose for moving us out of bondage. Jesus said, "Come unto me all ye that labor and are heavy laden, and I will give you rest; take my yoke upon you and learn of me, for I am meek and lowly of heart and you will find rest unto your souls. For my yoke is easy and my burden is light." Matthew 11:28,29.

God's liberation, His freedom is not to be free in and of yourself, but it is freedom in Him. His freedom is redemptive freedom. He frees us to be His light. He delivered Israel so that they could worship and serve Him. He freed them and us to be His people. God takes those who are downtrodden and uses us as peculiar treasure.

Every time I think about the Middle Passage, that horrendous voyage of the Atlantic Slave Trade from

> **Pharaoh thought he was god, but the Exodus, the crossing of the Red Sea, the guidance in the Wilderness, and the miraculous provision of food and water served to remind Pharaoh and Israel who God really is.**

the western coast of Africa to the Americas, where over one million Africans lost their lives and the remainder were sold into slavery, I see God's resolve. God had a plan and though we might not understand it completely, we must somehow resolve that God has a plan that cannot be quelled. Even after four hundred years of servitude, the lamp of God, the light of God, could not be extinguished in the Black race. No Pharaoh can stop the plans of God.

Pharaoh thought he was god, but the Exodus, the crossing of the Red Sea, the guidance in the Wilderness, and the miraculous provision of food and water served to remind Pharaoh and Israel who God really is. Every time I think about where I've come from, every time I think about the elders, every time I recall my grandparents, every time they tell me about my heritage and legacy, I thank God for being here. I thank God for being God who promised me a heritage.

This was the goal for which God was working as He commissioned Moses to confront Pharaoh. The great Exodus was done that Israel might enjoy the inheritance of the Promised Land. We were liberated and freed to be God's special people so that we might enjoy His heritage. And that's the legacy from which we proceed. We need to be in harmony with God. We need to know that God has a purpose for all of us.

God told Moses to tell Pharaoh that for this very purpose I raised you up. Even evil, powerful, and even bodacious men and women have to give attribution to God. God raised up Pharaoh for just that time and we need to know and not be undone when evil men come to power. God is still in control. God uses sometimes those of other persuasions to fulfill His purpose.

It doesn't matter who is in power. God's ultimate plan will be fulfilled. And the great joy is that His ultimate plan is that we be redeemed and live for Him. Isn't that something? Isn't that easy? Maybe not, because the world is so attractive and the lights and the glitter are so sedating, redemption becomes difficult.

But God proved His delivering power by bringing Israel through the Red Sea and the Wilderness, and if He did it for them, I know He will do it for us. In fact that's why God gave His Son as a guarantee for our deliverance. We can take comfort in His resolve to redeem us.

What a wonderful message! What a powerful truism that God did everything possible for us to live as His people. We are a mighty, mighty race and we ought to stand proudly and affirm our faith. God did what He did for our country through many who were castigated and pushed aside as nobodies. God in His infinite purpose and power used the elders, the men and women of African descent to get us here today. "Through many dangers, toils and snares we've already come." It was grace that brought us safe thus far, and if we go further, it will be grace that leads us on.

I was in Atlanta some time ago for Morehouse College Founders' Day. As I walked through the halls of the chapel, I gazed upon the portraits of those who had gone before us, who gave so much so that we could be who we are, I bowed my head in thankfulness.

Then as the ceremony began to close, Morehouse's Glee Club began to sing, "Got a mind to do Right". As those voices melded together and those brothers began to sing, it brought back memories. It was these words that captured my mind, "Got a mind to do right, got a mind; got a mind to live right, got a mind. Got a mind to serve right, got a mind, Jesus gave me this mind to do right."

That's true liberation. When we answer the call of God to be a light to the nation, when our testament corresponds to our lives, when we commit to being our best and doing our best, then Pharaoh will truly meet Great Jehovah.

When the Lord calls us to service, He's not concerned with what we do have or don't have; what God is concerned about is our willingness to allow our will to become one with His will.

Twin Towers, 144

Notes

Twin Towers, 145

God's Choice of Freedom for Oppressed People

Mighty tasks will be accomplished when we people of African descent are galvanized as a group. We, this grand cadre of people of the African Diaspora, when harnessed by God, will become lights to a dark world. The galvanizing process takes place through prophetic words like the ones under investigation in this text. "And they took their journey from Elim, and all the congregation of the children of Israel came unto the wilderness of Sin, which is between Elim and Sinai, on the fifteenth day of the second mouth after their departing out of the land of Egypt." Exodus 16:1.

> One of the sad commentaries of our community, the Black community, is that we get bogged down in our pilgrimage from slavery to freedom.

One of the sad commentaries of our community, the Black community, is that we get bogged down in our pilgrimage from slavery to freedom. History records that in our quest to Canaan, the Promised Land, there are things that have popped-up and obstacles that have come to impede our progress. Sometimes it's things that pop-up. Sometimes it's people who pop-up.

Sometimes the oppressor himself becomes the major obstacle in our quest for real and true freedom. Inherent in what has just been stated is the understanding that we are not yet fully free. We haven't made it to the Promised Land yet. Not realizing this essential point is part of the reason we find ourselves bogged down in a quagmire at times. We become sidetracked with the illusion of freedom.

This text reveals what many of us as sons and daughters of African descent have discovered about life, that freedom is real. God's demonstration of His ever-present power, presence and prominence to Pharaoh through Moses proved that freedom is real. Yet in our quest for freedom the illusion of what God really wants for us often bogs us down. God made a covenant with Israel's forefathers, Abraham, Isaac and Jacob that He would make of them a great nation and give them the Promised Land.

And what happened in Egypt, the Pharaoh that rose who knew not Joseph, the 400 years of enslavement, their harsh treatment was a part of the process God used for their freedom. Israel was actually being hardened for the road to come; they were being prepared for a life that would not be confused as a relaxed ride along life's merry-go-round. Egypt had gotten them ready for the rough journey ahead.

I applaud the African American businesses that have remained in the blighted inner cities of America. And I still have great admiration for those Black businesses that were once in our community but are on longer there. I applaud Black business because in the short life God has given me I've learned success in life doesn't come without a struggle. These Black businessmen and women have paid a high price for their financial freedom.

No matter the goal, no matter what we strive for, it doesn't come haphazardly or easily. There are no bright tomorrows without a little rain. You can't expect glorious paths without a few crooks in the road. There is no such thing as being the king of the hill without a few bumps and bruises. I've learned that anything worthwhile is worth staying the course for. History records that there are no accomplishments without some struggles, especially for sons and daughters of Africa.

Let me press that point further. Part of the problem in the African American community is that we have forgotten what it has taken to get where we are. It's sad but there are Black folks, people of the African Diaspora, who not only want to forget about our past, but want to completely disassociate themselves with our past struggle. The truth being told, however, in times of prosperity, like we are experiencing, there is the tendency for all of us to forget the sacrifices that were made. There is the illusion that we have arrived.

Yes, God has blessed us to be where we are, but we have not reached Canaan yet. If there are those who think we have arrived, this message is a reality check. Don't get confused about the process of liberation.

The text informs us that Israel was in the wilderness on their way to Canaan, but it wasn't a problem-less journey. It was a journey filled with bitter experiences along the way. Hunger and thirst reared their ugly heads turning their day of deliverance into a nightmare of fright. Their fear drove them to wish for the water and food that had while enslaved. Discouragement set in before they had hardly gotten started. Just a few days out of Egypt and they had forgotten the mighty work God had done on their behalf.

He had broken their chains, but fear and discouragement made them want to go back to make brick from mud just to eat a little meat. The cost of freedom was too much for them.

How many of us experienced those of our own households who have misappropriated the good news

> **Israel talked freedom but they thought slavery.**

and the good common sense that it takes to get from point A to point B? How many in our households, in our lineage who have misunderstood that task of becoming successful whether in business, medicine, law, or even as a pastor? How many do you know who just want success given to them? Think about this; how many of us have helped create dependency among our youth and others by giving them everything?

Israel talked freedom but they thought slavery. They started out watching God but they turned back to Pharaoh. Their eyes were on Canaan but their hearts were in Egypt.

We must be careful in the journey from slavery to freedom, we can't halt between two opinions. We must either decide to pay the price of freedom or return to slavery. There is no middle ground. God wants us to have real freedom. He wants us to experience freedom to the ultimate degree. But there are several things we've got to come to terms with in order to know God's choice of freedom and God's choice of freedom is different from ours.

First we have to know that our focus must be fixed. If we are going to really be free, the elders said it this way, "we've got to have a made-up mind." We must have a determination that we are going forward and nothing will deter us from moving forward. This was not the case for ancient Israel.

The text reveals that as soon as they hit the highway, they began to murmur against the leader. Their cry was, "we wish we would have died by the hand of God in Egypt; at least we would have had full stomachs."

Isn't it funny how we can live in the past? Don't get me wrong, I believe we should know our past and never be ashamed of it as African Americans. But we must never live in it. We must never try and go back and recapitulate the past. There may have been some good, good old days, but you still can't live there. And the truth is not all the good old days were good. There were some bad, good old days.

In the heat of the struggle, Israel thought about the little food in Egypt but forgot about the oppression. They wanted to go back to Egypt forgetting about their earlier cry to God because of Pharaoh's mistreatment. They forgot about the whips, the straw being taken, their women being ravaged, and their children being exploited. They were romanticizing their past. They were making the past look better than it really was.

Now you can't fault people for having a grand remembrance of the past especially when one reflects on God's miraculous preservation, provisions and protection. The problem comes when we romanticize the past making it more glamorous than it was.

Looking back on the past is good when it serves as a reminder and an impotence for moving forward, but we do ourselves harm and disavow who God is and what God's promise is for us when we romanticize the past with the wish of returning. Romanticizing the past leads to wasteful daydreaming.

How many times have you looked backwards when God was trying to take you forward? How many times have you focused on what was rather than on what is? How many times has the Lord placed in your spirit something to help you move ahead concerning an opportunity, job, business venture, or even a new spiritual level and you couldn't grasp it because you were bogged down in yesterday?

Have you ever talked with someone whose conversation was entirely about what they used to do?

Quite annoying. The question that comes up is, "What are you doing today?"

Most of us have gone to visit the place of our birth, our hometown. While there, you run into persons who obviously hadn't progressed. Their conversation quickly took a spin backward to events and places that you have long forgotten and don't really care to remember, but that's their heyday.

That's where they have chosen to live. God makes it clear that if we, especially the castigated and marginalized, are to experience the freedom He has chosen for us, we must reflect on the past but live in the present. We must fix our focus on that which is ahead and not what's in the past.

Living in the present means keeping our antennas up for the racial distorts that still plague our societies. I am a big proponent of educating our children about how to discern opposition that comes in friendly wardrobes. This illusion of freedom has fooled us and consequently has left our children ignorant of the struggle. Our young people have been fooled to believe that all you need to succeed in this country of ours is the right education, the right degree, the right job, live in the right place, and know the right people.

While that all is good and those things do play a part in one's success, but that alone won't get it. What many Black youth seem to not understand is that while Dr. King's dream of not being judged by the color of your skin but the content of your character is a wonderful idea, we as sons and daughters of Africa still are judged, by many, first by the color our skin.

> **What many Black youth seem to not understand is that while Dr. King's dream of not being judged by the color of your skin but the content of your character is a wonderful idea, we as sons and daughters of Africa still are judged, by many, first by the color our skin.**

Parents haven't inculcated the message into the minds of their children that it doesn't matter what you have, it doesn't matter how many degrees you have earned, when you go into that marketplace, you will have to work twice as hard; you still have to produce more than your counterpart. The reality is that you oftentimes still have to train your supervisor while your pay never changes and you still have to do twice as much to get the same recognition.

So often in our communities, young and old don't have the antennas our grandparents had that allow them to recognize the enemy where ever he was. It was the antennas that taught our grandmothers and grandfathers that there are some things you don't talk about in the marketplace. Their antennas kept them from falling for the illusion that Black folks would be accepted in the inner circle. It would do us well to replant those antennas in youth if we are to reach Canaan.

God's chosen freedom is predicated on a focus fixed on the future, a future the entails new leadership styles. If we are going to experience God's chosen freedom for oppressed people, our faith in leadership must be firm. This requires redefining leadership in the church and community. We must come to terms with the need for 21st century leadership methods.
There are many things we must hold on to but there is something we must include that are reflective of the 21st century and that is the notion of shared leadership. There are many reasons why our churches and communities are limping along, but I believe the major cause for the limp is antiquated leadership models. We still in many quadrants embrace leadership models that are personality driven rather than programmatically driven.

Even in the church, we pastors can't do it all and shouldn't be trying to do it all. Pastors shouldn't want to try to be all things to all people, especially at a time when there are so many skilled and spiritually mature lay-members in the pew of our churches who are anxious and desirous of helping build the kingdom. Shared leadership doesn't have to be all ordained. It doesn't have to come from the deacons and/or deaconesses, choir, or even assistant ministers. It comes from the pew and the empowerment of the laity. Shared leadership comes with the inclusion of women both ordained and non-ordained in ministry in areas of leadership that we aspire to reach.

In my many years in ministry, I have seen that we get bogged down because we are skewed on the issues of leadership. We embrace past leadership models and are afraid to move forward with new leadership models that will bring us to freedom. I do believe we've got to be more inclusive of our people when it comes to leadership, instead we grumble and complain like ancient Israel as God attempted to bring them to freedom.

Coming back to our text again in Exodus 16, the text says they murmured against Moses. Moses represented God; therefore in actuality the complaint was lodged against God not against Moses. Moses represents the first pastoral leader because Israel was known as the church in the wilderness. Moses represents the first model of leadership, the one-man-show model, later modified by his father-in-law Jethro. Jethro offered Moses some wise counsel, he said, "Moses you can't do it all by yourself. You've got to establish some leaders."

Like Moses, we must start trusting and putting our faith in leaders God sends us. We have seen too often splits and schisms in God's church and in our communities from the fall out over leadership. If we're going to experience real freedom, we must learn to put our trust in leaders we know have been sent by God. It is good to know that there are some great leaders surfacing in our churches and communities.

A biblical example of how God ferrets out leaders is in the Samuel commission to anoint a new king after Israel's first king Saul was rejected by God. Samuel was sent to the house of Jesse with the conviction that the king would come from among the men inside the home of Jesse. But after examining all the fine-looking sons of Jessie inside the house, none of them were chosen by God. Samuel then asked Jessie did he still have yet another son. Jessie responded, "Yes, I have a little straggly boy who is out in the field, but I know you don't want him. He's just a little lad, immature and still wet behind his ears."

When Samuel saw the son David, God said that's the one. We have got to have faith in new leaders that will come from unusual situations and circumstances. We must be willing and open to change some of our models creating new paradigms in our communities as God directs. God wants to lead us from our past to the present but in order to do that our faith in leadership must be firm. I'm convinced that our confidence in leadership will grow firm as we fix our focus on the future.

> We must be willing and open to change some of our models creating new paradigms in our communities as God directs.

Finally, If we're going to experience God's choice of freedom for oppressed people we must know that our future hope must be bound to our present past. Our future hope, our eschatological truth must be tied up with our existential present. God's promise to Israel was sure and certain. He didn't tell them they might receive the promise and they might reach Canaan. He told them I have a land that is carved out for you. It is a land flowing with milk and honey. It's a land of plenty. Everybody will have a share. Everybody will have their forty acres and a mule. Everybody can have their own home, their own chalet, and their own home in their chosen community. Everybody can have his or her own acreage because God promised it to us.

To know the freedom that comes with the fulfillment of the promise, you've got to know that His promise is tied to our present. Oftentimes what bogs us down is refusing to know that our future is linked with our present and our present with our past. In Deuteronomy 26 there is a marvelous story recorded by a young Israelite in response to a question posed about what to tell his children when they reach the land of promise. In the same response, we can tell our children in the years and months to come when they ask, why are you still obedient to God's rules and ordinances, why do still attend church and give tithe, why do you still give offerings, why are you still sacrificing your time to build programs, and why are you still stanch in your belief that God is the God of Abraham, Isaac, and Jacob and God is still the God of your future.

The scripture instructs us to tell them that we were once slaves down in Egypt. Pharaoh had his foot on our necks. We were mistreated and marginalized, counted as chattel slaves but the Lord with a mighty hand delivered us. The youthful Israelite recites,
"My father was a wandering Aramean, and he went down into Egypt with a few people and

> *lived there and became a great nation, powerful and numerous. But the Egyptians mistreated us and made us suffer, putting us to hard labor."* Deuteronomy 26:5,6.

The young Jew ends in a celebration, praising God for delivering His people. So we were slaves, were castigated and abused but God delivered us. He set us free. The point of the young Israelite's' story is that he considers himself a part of the saga. He tells the story as if he were there. It is evident his ancestors had passed on the story and he had claimed it, embraced it, as if he had participated in it. He included himself as a part of the story saying we were harshly treated and we were slaves.

This young Israelite understood that in order to get to the future his hope had to be bound to the reality of his frightening present, and the days of his gloomy past. But he also understood that he wouldn't be kept in the frightening present or gloomy past if he made the connection between the two. What makes us sure of reaching Canaan is knowing that the story is a whole story, that our past and present are linked to the future.

Seeing the whole picture allows us to connect the journey. So if you become despondent, if you become discouraged, if you ever become dissuaded, if you ever feel pressed down, know that God's future for you is sure. God's future is absolutely sure. Know that the same God who delivered Daniel from the lion's den and the three Hebrew boys from the fiery

> **Understand there are some things we are to leave in the past and press on toward the mark for the high calling in Christ Jesus.**

furnace will deliver us. Paul's words bring the hope, *"this one thing I do, forgetting those things which are behind."* Philippians 2:14.

Paul encourages us by suggesting that no matter where you are, no matter what you've experienced forget those things which are behind, forget those things that have bogged you down, forget those enemies who have attempted to ensnare you, forget the systematic evil that lurks near you. Understand there are some things we are to leave in the past and press on toward the mark for the high calling in Christ Jesus. I'm glad that God really does have freedom and that we can have that freedom if we connect with Him. So don't get bogged down. Know that freedom is real. Keep your focus fixed on the future and your faith firm in God sent leaders. Keep on pressing.

I know there are times when you get tired, times when you feel like quitting, times when you get tired of trudging and you get a little lax with your responsibilities, but just keep pressing on. You've got to press forward because others are counting on you, generation unborn are depending on you, so keep on pressing. God's people, his church, and our community are worth the sacrifice. Don't become disillusioned with life or dissuaded from the course. Let's keep on pressing. The hymn writer penned these words,

> *"I'm pressing on the upward way;*
> *new heights I'm gaining everyday,*
> *still praying as I onward bound;*
> *Lord, plant my feet on higher ground."*

We've got to press on. Our elders knew it well. They didn't give up though the vicissitudes of life pressed in against them. Where would we be now if the elders during the dark days of slavery had given up? So don't ever give up. God is still on our side and He will see us through.

Next Steps:
A Proactive Stance

> **The Church must really stand up now and be counted as willing to lead our country to the place of oneness.**

I believe firmly that if the Church would systematically address the issue of race and racism in this country, we could produce a model that those of other faith traditions and those of none would be willing to adopt and demonstrate as we lead America into authentic community. The Church can no longer be silent on the very issue that stained the documents this country forged at its inception. The Church must really stand up now and be counted as willing to lead our country to the place of oneness. Only we who believe in the power of reconciliation and healing can. In order to bring down the ominous twin towers or race and racism in America:

We must first be able to give an honest account of our political and economic stewardship as a nation under God

- Teach what the Nation's responsibility to God and to its citizens is
- Make a more definitive statement about what racism is
- Clearly understand why the Church must address the issue of racism as a Faith issue

- Examine with historical accuracy the eras of Slavery, Reconstruction, and Civil Rights in an effort to have them formally acknowledged and embraced by America (academically, economically, and politically) as integral to life and livelihood in America

Next we must wisely acknowledge the "useable past" or truth of our history in America
- Insist that it is only the truth of God that makes us truly free
- Create institutions where wisdom is employed to teach the importance of cultural relevance
- Use Acts of The Apostles as a teaching tool to compare and contrast America's history
- Produce and publish biblically and morally sound books/documents of America's past

Lastly, we must allow our "useable past" to reshape and represent ourselves and our resources as to insure a bright and vibrant future for all Americans
- Believe it is possible to dismantle racism in America
- Believe that together we can create a new vision and a new hope for this country
- Believe that eradicating racism will lead to more institutional expressions of the universal church

Twin Towers, 166

- Believe that producing anti-racist/multi-cultural churches to be the most pivotal step in the process of dismantling racism for the United States.

About the Author

Reverend Alfred M. Walker serves presently as Chaplain with Baylor Health Care System at the Baylor University Medical Center, and the Diabetes Health and Wellness Institute in Dallas, Texas. Reverend Walker served as the Senior Pastor of the historic New Hope Baptist Church in Dallas, Texas. Before coming to Dallas, Reverend Walker served as pastor of Liberty Baptist Church in Augusta, Georgia.

Reverend Walker received his Bachelor of Arts degree from Morehouse College in Atlanta, Georgia, and Master of Divinity degree from Morehouse School of Religion at the Interdenominational Theological Center also, in Atlanta, Georgia. He is presently a candidate for the Doctor of Ministry degree.

Rev. Walker served three years as a petty officer in the United States Navy. His community involvement has been extensive over the years serving as President of the Augusta, Georgia, NAACP, President of the University Hospital Clergy Staff, as a member of Sun Trust Bank Advisory Board, and many others. While here in Dallas, Rev. Walker has served as a member the African American Pastors' Coalition (Chairman, Political Action Committee), a member of the Board of Directors of the Metro Dallas Homeless Alliance, Greater Dallas Community of Churches, and as a Board Member of the St. Philips School & Community Center.

Rev. Walker is married to Angela Bedford Walker. They are the proud parents of two children, Azaria Ruth and Alfred Mark. His daughter Aisha Renae Walker completes his family.

Also from Searchlight Press

Developing Oneness in Marriage:
A 'How-to' for Husbands
by Rev. Dr. Lloyd C. Blue
(Searchlight Press, 2011)

Character Is Key:
In Sports and in Life
by Eddie Hill and Dr. Jim Moore
(Searchlight Press, 2010)

Headed the Wrong Direction?
Calling Us and Others
Back from the Edge
by Rev. Wade J. Simmons
(Searchlight Press, 2011)

Wonderworking Power:
A Fresh Translation
of the Gospel of Mark
by John Cunyus
(Searchlight Press, 2011)

Twin Towers, 170

The Way of Wisdom:
Job, Proverbs, Ecclesiastes,
Song of Solomon
by John Cunyus
(Searchlight Press, 2008)

The Audacity of Prayer:
A Fresh Translation of the Book of Psalms
by John Cunyus
(Searchlight Press, 2009)

The Latin Torah:
Genesis, Exodus, Leviticus, Numbers,
Deuteronomy
by John Cunyus
(Searchlight Press, 2010)

Searchlight Press
Who are you looking for?
Publishers of thoughtful Christian books since 1994.
5634 Ledgestone Drive
Dallas, TX 75214-2026
888.896.6081
info@Searchlight-Press.com
www.Searchlight-Press.com